Acknowledgements

Photographs from www.crocstockimages.com, www.careimages.com, www.thepowerofpositiveimages.com, www.shutterstock.com and Photosymbols.

A selection of images used by kind permission of: Chubb Fire & Security; Safe Fire Direct; Department of Health in association with the Welsh Assembly Government; the Scottish Government; the Food Standards Agency in Northern Ireland.

Our thanks to Caroline, Christine, Lois, Sophie, Choices Housing and Autism Plus for their help.

Study skills

Studying for a qualification can be very rewarding. However, it can be daunting if you have not studied for a long time, or are wondering how to fit your studies into an already busy life. The BILD website contains lots of advice to help you to study successfully, including information about effective reading, taking notes, organising your time, and using the internet for research. For further information, go to www.bild.org.uk/qualifications

Contents

Acknowledgements   vi

About the author and the people who contributed to this book   vii

Introduction   ix

Chapter 1:   Health and safety in the work setting   1

Chapter 2:   Understanding and managing risk   19

Chapter 3:   Responding to accidents and sudden illness   33

Chapter 4:   Medication and health care tasks   50

Chapter 5:   Reducing the spread of infection   61

Chapter 6:   Food safety, nutrition and hydration   73

Chapter 7:   Safe moving and positioning   88

Chapter 8:   Handling hazardous substances and materials   99

Chapter 9:   Fire safety in the work setting   108

Chapter 10:   Security measures in the work setting   129

Chapter 11:   Managing stress   148

Glossary   159

Index   164

This book covers:

- Common Induction Standards – Standard 8 – Health and safety in an adult social care setting
- The level 2 diploma unit HSC 027 – Contribute to health and safety in health and social care
- The level 3 diploma unit HSC 037 – Promote and implement health and safety in health and social care

Health and safety
for learning disability workers

Series Editor: Lesley Barcham

Mandatory unit and Common Induction Standards titles

Communicating effectively with people with a learning disability
ISBN 978 0 85725 510 5

Personal development for learning disability workers ISBN 978 0 85725 609 6

Equality and inclusion for learning disability workers ISBN 978 0 85725 514 3

Duty of care for learning disability workers ISBN 978 0 85725 613 3

Principles of safeguarding and protection for learning disability workers
ISBN 978 0 85725 506 8

Person centred approaches when supporting people with a learning disability
ISBN 978 0 85725 625 6

The role of the learning disability worker ISBN 978 0 85725 637 9

Handling information for learning disability workers ISBN 978 0 85725 633 1

Health and safety for learning disability workers ISBN 978 0 85725 641 6

Titles supporting a unit from the level 2 health and social care qualifications

An introduction to supporting people with autistic spectrum conditions
ISBN 978 0 85725 710 7

An introduction to supporting people with a learning disability
ISBN 978 0 85725 709 3

Titles supporting a unit from the level 3 health and social care qualifications

Promoting positive behaviour when supporting people with a learning
disability and people with autism ISBN 978 0 85725 713 0

Next steps in supporting people with autistic spectrum conditions
ISBN 978 0 85275 705 5

Health and safety for learning disability workers

Alice Bradley

Supporting the level 2 and 3 diplomas in
Health and Social Care (learning disability pathway)
and the Common Induction Standards

LearningMatters

bild
all about people

SAGE | **LearningMatters**

bild
all about people

Learning Matters
An imprint of SAGE Publications Ltd
1 Oliver's Yard
55 City Road
London EC1Y 1SP

SAGE Publications Inc.
2455 Teller Road
Thousand Oaks, California 91320

SAGE Publications India Pvt Ltd
B 1/I 1 Mohan Cooperative Industrial Area
Mathura Road
New Delhi 110 044

SAGE Publications Asia-Pacific Pte Ltd
3 Church Street
#10–04 Samsung Hub
Singapore 049483

Editor: Luke Block
Production controller: Chris Marke
Project management: Deer Park Productions
Marketing manager: Tamara Navaratnam
Cover design: Pentacor
Typeset by: Pantek Media, Maidstone, Kent
Printed by: Ashford Colour Press, Gosport, Hants

BILD
Campion House
Green Street
Kidderminster
Worcestershire
DY10 1JL
© 2013 BILD

First published in 2013 jointly by Learning Matters Ltd
and the British Institute of Learning Disabilities.

British Library Cataloguing in Publication Data

A catalogue record for this book is available from the
British Library

ISBN 978 0 85725 641 6 (pbk)

ISBN 978 0 85725 841 0

FSC
www.fsc.org

MIX
Paper from
responsible sources
FSC® C011748

About the authors and the people who contributed to this book

Alice Bradley

Alice Bradley has been working with people with learning disabilities and families for many years. She has lived and worked in the UK, Canada and Thailand in schools, universities, health and community settings, as well as in international development in several countries in Africa and Asia. She has a particular interest in inclusion, empowerment and the support of people with profound and multiple learning disabilities. She lives near Hamilton in Scotland.

Linda Campbell

Linda Campbell has worked with people with a learning disability as an advocate, self advocacy trainer and coordinator of self advocacy groups for the last 13 years. She supports people with a learning disability to deliver training on self advocacy, anti bullying, values and health and safety. She has a keen interest in self directed support. Linda also supports the families of young people with profound and multiple learning disabilities who are approaching transition from school to adult services. She previously managed a multi-cultural community centre.

Caroline Dawson

Caroline Dawson lives in her own house in Linwood, near Paisley. She is a co-trainer with Enable and focuses on values in the induction of new workers. Caroline has support for housework, paying bills, preparing meals, going shopping and medication. Because Caroline is blind she uses a cane to get around in the community. She learned Braille at school in Edinburgh and went on to college in England where she studied life skills and computing. Caroline enjoys going to the gym, working on the computer, swimming, going to drama and listening to music.

Christine Higgins

Christine Higgins lives in Glasgow. She employs her own personal care assistants through funding from the Independent Living Fund. They support her with her daily routines of getting up in the morning and going to bed at night. Neither of her workers has had previous experience with disabled people so she is the first person to have provided them with training. Christine uses an electric wheelchair and her house is adapted to help her maintain her independence. She is involved in a variety of activities outside the home. She previously had a part-time job as a library assistant in a higher education institution and has obtained a qualification in computing.

Introduction

Who this book is for

Health and Safety for Learning Disability Workers is for you if you:

- have a new job working with people with learning disabilities with a support provider or as a personal assistant;

- are a more experienced worker who is studying for a qualification for your own professional development or are seeking more information to improve your practice;

- are a volunteer supporting people with a learning disability;

- are a manager in a service supporting people with a learning disability and you have training or supervisory responsibility for the induction of new workers and the continuous professional development of more experienced staff;

- are a direct payment or personal budget user and are planning the induction or training for your personal assistant.

Links to qualifications and the Common Induction Standards

This book gives you all the information you need to complete both the Common Induction Standard on health and safety, and the unit on promoting health and safety from the level 2 and level 3 diplomas in health and social care. You may use the learning from this unit in a number of ways:

- to help you complete the Common Induction Standards;

- to work towards a full qualification e.g. the level 2 or level 3 diploma in health and social care;

- as learning for the unit on health and safety for your professional development.

This unit is one of the mandatory units that everyone doing the full level 2 and level 3 diploma must study. Although anyone studying for the qualifications will find the book useful, it is particularly helpful for people who support a person with a learning disability. The messages and stories used in this book are from people with a learning disability, family carers and people working with them.

Links to assessment

If you are studying for this unit and want to gain accreditation towards a qualification, first of all you will need to make sure that you are registered with an awarding organisation which offers the qualification. Then you will need to provide a portfolio of evidence for assessment. The person responsible for training within your organisation will advise you about registering with an awarding organisation and give you information about the type of evidence you will need to provide for assessment. You can also get additional information from BILD. For more information about qualifications and assessment, go to the BILD website: www.bild.org.uk/qualifications

How this book is organised

Generally each chapter covers one learning outcome from the qualification unit, and one of the Common Induction Standards. The learning outcomes covered are clearly highlighted at the beginning of each chapter. Each chapter starts with a story from a person with a learning disability or family carer or worker. This introduces the topic and is intended to help you think about the topic from their point of view. Each chapter contains:

 Thinking points – to help you reflect on your practice;

Stories – examples of good support from people with learning disabilities and family carers;

 Activities – for you to use to help you to think about your work with people with learning disabilities;

Key points – a summary of the main messages in that chapter;

References and where to go for more information – useful references to help further study.

At the end of the book there is:

A glossary – explaining specialist language in plain English;

An index – to help you look up a particular topic easily.

Chapter 1

Health and safety in the work setting

John, who is in his 70s, lives in a flat in a housing complex for people with learning disabilities. Like most of us, he values and guards his independence. He knows his neighbourhood well, he has lived there for over twenty years and is accustomed to using all local facilities, mainly on his own, but with help if he requests it. Recently however, he's become a bit more unsteady and somewhat forgetful. He's been brought home by different local people three times after falling, though he wasn't badly hurt.

His support staff are becoming concerned and know that they need to review the situation, but are also aware of the balance between providing support, which will keep him safe, and limiting his independence and intruding into his lifestyle.

Agnes lives in the same complex as John, but in accommodation shared with three other people. She's been desperate to get her own flat for several years and has been told that it will happen, but there haven't been any suitable vacancies. Agnes has quite complex health needs, which have increased substantially over recent months and include diabetes, impaired mobility and vision. There are differences of opinion amongst the staff who support Agnes. Some think she should stay in the group situation while others think she should still be given the chance to have her own place.

Introduction

Situations like those described above are fairly common and can cause dilemmas for support workers. On the one hand, you want to make sure that people with learning disabilities have every opportunity for living their lives the way they want to. On the other hand, there's your responsibility for the safety and wellbeing of the person or people you support.

Being fully informed about your own responsibilities and those of others in relation to health and safety will not only help you keep yourself and other people safe and well, but will also enable you to do your work with greater peace of mind.

Learning outcomes

This chapter will help you to:

- become familiar with the legislation relating to health and safety in your work situation;

- understand and explain the *policies and procedures* or *ways of working* agreed with your employer;

- become more aware of your own responsibilities with regard to health and safety, those of your manager and of the person or people you support;

- identify what you can and cannot do in relation to health and safety at your current stage of training;

- find out where and from whom you can access additional support and information in relation to health and safety.

This chapter covers:

Common Induction Standards – Standard 8 – Health and safety in an adult social care setting: Learning Outcome 1

Level 2 HSC 027 – Contribute to health and safety in health and social care: Learning Outcome 1

Level 3 HSC 037 – Promote and implement health and safety in health and social care: Learning Outcome 1

Health and safety legislation in a health or social care work setting

Health and safety legislation in the UK

The health and safety legislation discussed in this book applies to all four nations of the United Kingdom unless stated otherwise. Where a particular piece of legislation does not apply to all parts of the UK, this is made explicit and the alternative legislation relevant to the particular nations of the UK is identified.

> All workers have a right to work in places where risks to their health and safety are properly controlled. Health and safety is about stopping you getting hurt at work or ill through work. Your employer is responsible for health and safety, but you must help.
>
> *Health and Safety Executive* www.hse.gov.uk/pubns/law.pdf

You and your employer carry legal responsibilities for health and safety at work, as does the person or people you support, insofar as they have the capacity to understand this responsibility.

The key piece of legislation you need to know about is the Health and Safety at Work Act (HSW) 1974 which sets out the responsibilities for everyone concerned: the employer, employees and others in or affected by the work setting.

The Health and Safety at Work Act 1974

The purpose of this Act is to promote and encourage high standards of health and safety at work, to protect employers and employees and anyone else affected by their work activities. In health and social care settings this would involve relatives, visiting professionals, contractors and so on. The Act covers all settings in which you work and all activities you are responsible for in your work role.

Under the Act your employer has a duty to ensure, as far as is reasonably practicable, the health, safety and welfare of all employees. This includes:

- protecting your health and safety;

- protecting the health and safety of others who might be affected by the work activities carried out in your work setting, for example the people who use the service, visitors, contractors, etc.;

- developing health and safety policies and ways of carrying them out, if employing more than five people.

As an employee you have a responsibility to:

- take care of your own health and safety and that of others;

- cooperate with your employer in all aspects of health and safety.

The Health and Safety at Work Act covers a very broad range of topics so a number of other pieces of legislation have been developed around it to deal with more specific aspects of health and safety in the workplace. These are known as regulations and they provide the detail required to make sure all the settings where people work and all workplace activities are as safe as possible, e.g. factories as well as residential care homes, safe handling of equipment and machinery, the prevention of accidents and the spread of infection and so on. Some of these regulations have more relevance for the kind of job you do than others.

The regulations which are most relevant to adult health and social care settings are:

- Health and Safety First Aid Regulations 1981

- Manual Handling Operations Regulations 1992

- Workplace (Health, Safety and Welfare) Regulations 1992

- Personal Protective Equipment at Work Regulations 1992

- Reporting of Injuries, Diseases and Dangerous Occurrences Regulation 1995 (RIDDOR)

- Provision and Use of Work Equipment Regulations 1998

- Lifting Operations and Lifting Equipment Regulations 1998 (LOLER)

- Provision and Use of Work Equipment Regulations 1998 (PUWER)

- Management of Health and Safety at Work Regulations 1999 (MHSWR)

- Control of Substances Hazardous to Health Regulations 2002

- Control of Substances Hazardous to Health (Amendment) Regulations 2003 (COSHH)

- England and Wales: Regulatory Reform (Fire Safety) Order 2005; Scotland: The Fire Scotland Act 2005 and Fire Safety (Scotland) Regulations 2006; Northern Ireland: Fire Safety Regulations (Northern Ireland) 2010

It's a long list but don't worry – you don't need to know all the details. You'll be learning more about them as you go through this book. In fact, you probably know quite a bit already. The clearer you are about health and safety in your own work setting, the more likely you are to keep yourself and others safe. Check out your own knowledge of health and safety in the activity below.

Activity

First, go through the questions below on your own.

- *What kind of health and safety training do you need to do so that you can carry out your own responsibilities? What have you done already?*
- *What kind of training do you need to do if you use special equipment like slide sheets or hoists?*
- *Why does health and safety training have to be updated regularly?*

Second, discuss your answers with your line manager at your next supervision.

How did you get on? Look back at the list of regulations and see which ones match what you have said. Some of the names give better clues than others as to what they are about, don't they?

Shared responsibilities for health and safety in health and social care settings

The Health and Safety Executive (HSE) is the national independent regulator for health and safety in the workplace, including publicly and privately owned health and social care settings in the UK. The HSE works in partnership with other bodies which regulate care.

In England, the Care Quality Commission (CQC) is the independent regulator of health and social care. CQC register and licence care services under the

Health and Social Care Act 2009 and associated regulations. They assess and monitor standards using the *Essential Standards of Quality and Safety*.

In Scotland, regulation and inspection is the responsibility of the Care Inspectorate for social care and Healthcare Improvement Scotland for health care.

In Wales, responsibility is with the Care and Social Services Inspectorate Wales for social care and the Healthcare Inspectorate Wales for health care.

Regulation in Northern Ireland is the responsibility of the Regulation and Quality Improvement Authority.

These care regulators have responsibility, with the Health and Safety Executive, for ensuring that health and safety policies and procedures are of a suitable standard in health and social care settings.

If you would like to find out more about the regulating body for your part of the UK, log on to www.hse.gov.uk/healthservices/arrangements.htm

Policies and procedures and agreed ways of working

Employers need to apply health and safety legislation in ways that are suitable for their particular work setting and the type of work involved. Nowadays adults with learning disabilities are supported in a wider range of situations than ever before: in communal settings such as residential or nursing homes and day centres; in short break services; in educational settings like colleges; in places of employment, whether paid or voluntary; in their own homes, where support is provided by an organisation or where the person him or herself, or a relative, is the employer. Some support workers work in a variety of places. So the ways in which health and safety legislation is put into practice in one setting, such as a day centre, will be very different from how it is applied in someone's own home.

Policies and procedures

Some settings will have formal policies and procedures; others will have less formal guidelines often known as agreed ways of working, while some may have a combination of both.

Written policies and procedures are required in organisations which employ more than five people. *Policies* set out the employer's commitment to health and safety in the particular work setting. *Procedures* specify in greater detail how health and safety policy will be implemented in the organisation, including specific responsibilities, accountability, methods of implementing the policy, monitoring and recording arrangements and what to do if there are difficulties. Employers are legally required to communicate this information to all employees.

Policies and procedures should cover all health and safety considerations relevant to that organisation and which are required by law. They should:

- set out the organisation's commitment to health and safety;

- describe how health and safety will be managed across the organisation, i.e. how the policy will be implemented;

- outline who has responsibility for the different aspects of health and safety;

- explain how particular activities will be managed, e.g. evacuation of premises, storage of hazardous materials, etc.

It is important to follow the policies and procedures of your organisation.

If you support someone in their own home, the ways in which health and safety requirements are undertaken will depend on who your employer is. Here are some examples.

If the person you support (or his or her relative) employs you through a direct payment or individual budget, the person managing the budget is your employer and has a responsibility to provide you with a safe work setting. You in turn have a responsibility for your own safety and that of the person you support and any others involved. You wouldn't necessarily expect to have formal written policies, but you would have agreed ways of working based on the person's support plan and worked out with him, her or the person managing the budget. You also have the responsibility to understand and follow the agreed ways of working. Risk assessment and support planning will have been undertaken prior to the individual budget or direct payment being approved. People who employ support workers in their own home must also have employers' liability insurance.

If the person employs you through an agency or organisation, the agency or organisation has health and safety responsibilities, but so do both you and the person you support. So you might have formal policies and procedures from the agency but perhaps also ways of working agreed between you and the person you support or a carer.

If you're employed in domiciliary work by the local council or a care provider, your employer must have formal written policies and procedures which you must be informed about and follow.

In situations where there are fewer than five employees, there is no requirement to have a written policy document, but it is good practice for agreed ways of working to be recorded, so that there is no confusion.

In most situations, the person with a learning disability will employ more than one support worker, so it is important that everyone involved is clear about the agreed ways of working that apply to health and safety.

The main points covered in policies and procedures and agreed ways of working

Policies and procedures in services for people with learning disabilities are likely to cover the following main points:

- the names of key people with responsibility for different aspects of health and safety;
- significant risks and risk assessments associated with them;

- how to move and position people safely;
- arrangements for emergencies such as fire and accidents;
- reporting procedures for accidents and sudden illness;
- how to handle and store hazardous substances;
- how to use equipment safely;
- methods of informing people about health and safety;
- arrangements for first aid.

If you are working in someone's home, most or all of these points will also be covered, but are likely to be expressed less formally and probably be less detailed, depending on the situation and the person's needs. For example, they might include:

- what support the person requires and how this should be provided;
- ways of maintaining safety in tasks where there are health and safety risks;
- what to do in emergency situations;
- any training required and who will provide it;
- when and how to monitor, review, update and amend the agreed ways of working.

Activity

Either:

If you are employed in an organisation, spend a bit of time reading your employer's health and safety policies and procedures. Then answer these questions:

- *Are there any points you don't understand? If so, who can you ask about these?*
- *Who would you go to if you had any questions or concerns about any aspect of health and safety?*
- *How can these policies and procedures help ensure your safety and that of the people you support?*

▶

Or:

If you are employed directly by someone with a learning disability, or the person's main carer, discuss with this person the main points covered by the health and safety agreements which are in place. (These may not be called 'health and safety' in the person's support plan but they'll be about things like medication, keeping safe, etc.) Here are suggestions for points you might cover:

- *Why are these particular issues important?*
- *How well are the agreements working?*
- *Are any additions, amendments or clarifications needed?*

Your employer's responsibilities for health and safety

Employers have a responsibility to make sure all employees are familiar with their health and safety policies and/or agreed ways of working. They also need to update and revise the policy regularly to keep pace with any changes in the service, the law or the needs of the people they support. Information must be presented in ways that are relevant and accessible to all employees. This might involve different languages and/or different formats. Policies, procedures and information must reflect equal opportunity and anti-discrimination practice in terms of gender, ethnicity and disability. Your employer must also provide you with appropriate health and safety training which should be designed for the situation in which you work and the particular needs of the people with learning disabilities you support.

Your employer's main responsibilities under the Health and Safety at Work Act 1974 are to:

- provide and maintain safe plant (machinery and equipment) and safe systems and practices;
- make arrangements for the safe handling, storage and transportation of all materials;
- provide employees with information, instruction, training and supervision as is necessary to ensure their health and safety at work;
- report accidents and injuries at work;
- provide a safe place of work with a safe entrance and exit;
- provide a safe working environment with adequate welfare facilities.

Where you are employed directly by someone with a learning disability

Health and safety guidance states that if you are employed directly by a person who has a learning disability, their home is your workplace and needs to be a safe environment for you to work in, as well as a safe and healthy environment for themselves. People who directly employ personal assistants and support workers should satisfy the local authority which funds their support that they are aware of health and safety as it affects them, anyone they employ and anyone else who is affected by the way in which their support is delivered. The person you support will have undergone a thorough care assessment and risk assessment process to ensure that any health and safety issues are taken into account. This then enables the person to take steps to minimise any potential risks to their support staff.

People employing their own support workers should provide information, training and, where required, supervision. This might include instruction on the use of any specific equipment such as hoists, moving and handling arrangements, particular food requirements, information about intimate care and dietary needs and other relevant areas.

People employing their own support workers should provide information, training and, where required, supervision.

If the person has contracted with a care organisation to provide his or her support, that organisation has prime responsibility for your health and safety, although the person concerned, and where relevant the relative, also bears responsibility for ensuring your safety. The organisation's managers should make clear to you where the responsibilities lie.

You will need to be aware of all the potential health and safety risks that may arise, be proactive in preventing any problems and be aware of what you need to do if you identify any risks or hazards in the home, e.g. trailing wires, a faulty boiler, obstacles, etc.

Your responsibility for health and safety

Under the Health and Safety at Work Act 1974, as an employee you have a responsibility to:

- cooperate with your employer on all health and safety matters;

- take reasonable care of your own health and safety and that of others who may be affected by your acts or omissions (this includes the people you support, your colleagues and any visitors to your workplace);

- work in accordance with all the training and the policies and procedures given to you by your employer;

- report any unsafe situations or equipment;

- report any injuries, strains or illnesses you receive as a result of carrying out your work;

- ensure you do not intentionally or recklessly damage or misuse any materials or equipment provided by your employer.

Breaching the health and safety legislation is a criminal offence which may lead to prosecution, a fine and up to two years in prison.

The health and safety responsibilities of the people you support

The person/s you support have health and safety responsibilities too. These include:

- looking after their own health and safety;

- ensuring that their actions do not have a negative impact or affect the safety of others, including support workers.

The extent to which people with learning disabilities will understand these responsibilities will vary according to their capacity to understand and carry out their responsibilities in general. As a support worker, you need to take account of this and use accessible and relevant ways of communicating information about their responsibilities, e.g. through regular discussion, reinforcing the information in situations that could be hazardous, drawing attention to things they do well to uphold health and safety, providing training and so on. Where people communicate in ways other than, or supplementary to, speech, for instance through signs, symbols and pictures, you need to make use of these in conveying information. This will ensure that the person/s you support can take responsibility for their own safety and wellbeing, and that of others.

If you work with people with profound and multiple learning disabilities it is important to be clear of the extent to which they are aware of safety and potential hazards. The best people to advise you are the person's closest family members and other workers who know them well. As you get to know the person better, you will have a clearer idea of their level of understanding and be able to adapt your support accordingly.

Thinking point

Is there anything you're unclear about in relation to your employer's responsibilities for your health and safety, your own responsibilities or those of the person/s you support? Who can you ask about this?

What you can and cannot do at each stage of your training

Your employer has a duty to provide information, instruction, training and appropriate supervision to protect you from hazards and risks. All health and safety training should be tailored to suit the particular setting in which you work and the needs of the people with learning disabilities whom you support in this work setting.

This training should include:

- an induction programme for new workers;
- instruction and supervision relating to all health and safety issues in your work setting, with particular relevance to the nature of that setting and the needs of the people being supported.

If you are employed by an organisation, the organisation has responsibility for your training and supervision. If you are employed by the person you support or a relative, that person should provide you with the necessary training and supervision where relevant.

To comply with health and safety law, you need to be aware of what you can and cannot do at each stage of your training. Undertaking tasks for which you have not been trained is dangerous and can put you and other people at risk.

Examples of activities you are not allowed to undertake until you have had the correct training include such things as:

- moving and positioning;

- giving medication;

- dealing with specialist health tasks, e.g. colostomy, ileostomy, peg feeding, giving injections;

- giving emergency first aid;

- using moving and handling equipment, e.g. hoists, stand-aids, transfer boards, slide sheets, etc.;

- undertaking risk assessments.

Health and safety training is regularly updated so you will need to attend regular refresher courses to make sure that your practice is up to date. You may also need additional training if anything changes in your job.

Where you are employed directly by the person you support, some of your training will be on the job and provided by the person you support or a carer. But there may be other areas for which you require specialised training, such as moving and positioning, using specialised equipment, managing medication or specialist feeding. This training should be written into the person's support plan and included in their budget. Where you feel you require additional training before undertaking certain tasks, you should discuss this with your employer and together seek support from the relevant person, who may be the person responsible for developing the support plan and/or agreeing the budget.

No matter how confident or competent you feel in your job, you must be aware that your health and safety, and that of the people you support and others, are of vital importance.

Do not undertake any task, use any equipment or carry out any procedure until you have been trained to do so and have all the necessary information at hand to enable the task to be safely undertaken. In attempting to do a good job you could breach the law and injure yourself or others.

Activity

Write down a list of all the health and safety training you have received to date and what you are qualified to do as a result of this training.

Look back at what you have written and then list any difficulties or concerns you have in carrying out the tasks you have been trained to do.

Do you need further training for these tasks?

Who do you need to talk to about this?

What else do you do in your work that you need training for?

Do you know when you will get this training? If not, who can you ask?

Once you have completed this activity discuss it with your line manager or other person who employs you.

Additional support, information and training

If you have any concerns and questions about health and safety, do you know who to go to for help and information? In an organisation you should approach your line manager or someone with specific health and safety responsibilities.

If you are employed directly by someone with a learning disability, or a relative who manages their budget, any safety issues or concerns will obviously be discussed between you in the first instance, but you might have to seek outside help, so you need to know who to ask for specialist advice.

Other people who can provide additional information and support

Local authorities employ a number of people who can provide advice and information, such as health and safety officers, environmental health officers and occupational health practitioners who are there to help with health and safety matters.

You can also get information from the Health and Safety Executive (HSE). You might like to look now at their website to get an idea of the very wide aspects of health and safety they cover: www.hse.gov.uk

Think about the different tasks you do in the course of your work. Are there things that occur to you about your own health and safety or those of others? Do you ever wonder about any of your own responsibilities to the person/s you support, or your employer's responsibilities to you? Who could you go to if you wanted to discuss any questions or concerns?

Key points from this chapter

- The main piece of legislation covering health and safety in work settings, including health and social care, is the Health and Safety at Work Act 1974. This legislation is complemented by a number of regulations that cover all relevant aspects of health and safety in health and social care settings.

- Health and safety policies and procedures should cover risk assessments and control measures associated with all aspects of your work setting and all activities undertaken in the course of the work.

- Your employer has a responsibility under the Health and Safety at Work Act, as far as is reasonably practicable, to ensure the health and safety of all employees, people with learning disabilities and anyone else affected by the work setting or activities.

- You have a responsibility to keep yourself and others safe, to comply with your employer's policies and procedures and/or agreed ways of working and to report any additional risks or hazards.

- The people you support have a responsibility, insofar as they have the capacity to understand, to keep themselves safe and not to put anyone else at risk.

- You should never undertake tasks which require specialised training until you have received the training. This might include moving and positioning, using specialist equipment, giving medication, first aid, risk assessment and specialist health tasks.

- You can obtain additional information about health and safety from your line manager, your workplace health and safety representative, the Health and Safety Executive or your local authority.

References and where to go for more information

References

Barksby, J and Harper, L (2011) *Duty of Care for Learning Disability Workers.* Exeter: Learning Matters/BILD

Fish Insurance (2006) *Safety Guide for Personal Assistants. An Essential Guide to Protect Employees Providing Support.* Available at: www.fishinsurance.co.uk

Health and Safety Executive (2001) *Health and Safety in Care Homes.* Available at: www.hse.gov.uk

Health and Safety Executive (2009) *Health and Safety Law. What you need to know.* Available at: www.hse.gov.uk

Health and Safety Executive (2012) *Who Regulates Health and Social Care.* Available at: www.hse.gov.uk

Mencap (2012) *Health: Legislation, Research and Good Practice.* Available at: www.mencap.org.uk

Mencap (2012) *Standards of Care: Legislation, Research and Good Practice.* Available at: www.mencap.org.uk

Shaw Trust Direct Payments Support Services (2007) *Information Sheet 8: Training your Personal Assistant.* Available at: www.shaw-trust.org.uk

Skills for Care (2009) *Toolkit to Help People Employ their Own Personal Assistants.* Available at: www.skillsforcare.org.uk

Websites

Care and Social Services Inspectorate Wales
www.csiw.wales.gov.uk

Care Inspectorate (Scotland) www.scswis.com

Care Quality Commission (England) www.cqc.org.uk

Health and Safety Executive www.hse.gov.uk

Health Care Inspectorate Wales www.hiw.org.uk

Healthcare Improvement Scotland
www.healthcareimprovementscotland.org

Regulation and Quality Improvement Authority (Northern Ireland) www.rqia.org.uk

Scottish Consortium for Learning Disabilities www.scld.org.uk

Chapter 2

Understanding and managing risk

Christine, who has cerebral palsy and uses an electric wheelchair, says:

'Snowboarding was always something I wanted to do, but it felt like a distant dream that could never happen because of my disability. But the dream came true and it gave me the best experience of my life so far.

Another 'problem' that occurred to me was that people said I wouldn't be able to go into employment because of my disability. Again I proved these people wrong as with support and guidance I started work at the college as a library assistant. Those four hours a week gave me the confidence I needed to know [that,] if I have faith in myself my disability shouldn't hold me back.'

The Management of Health and Safety at Work Regulations 1999 places a duty on employers to assess and manage risks to their employees and others arising from work activities.

www.healthyworkinglives.com

Being risk averse has resulted in some frontline practitioners making decisions about direct payments for people based on generalised views about the capacity or 'riskiness' of certain groups ... rather than making decisions with the individual with an understanding of their circumstances.

Enabling Risk, Ensuring Safety: Self Directed Support and Personal Budgets
www.scie.org.uk

Introduction

Christine's snowboarding and employment experiences and the two quotations at the beginning of this chapter highlight a thorny subject in the lives of people with learning disabilities and support workers – the challenge of risk. On the one hand, as a support worker, you are committed to helping people achieve the lifestyles they want, promoting empowerment, self-determination and decision making. On the other hand you need to balance this with your duty of care and your legal responsibility to protect people from unnecessary risk and ensure their safety. Risk is present in all our lives and unavoidable. By addressing risk directly, assessing its likelihood and possible consequences, we can put in place measures that will help us and the people we support manage it more effectively.

Learning outcomes

This chapter will help you to:

- understand the importance of assessing health and safety risks posed by the work setting or particular activities;
- learn about monitoring and reporting health and safety risks;
- learn about health and safety risk assessments;
- develop ways to minimise potential risks and hazards;
- understand how risk assessment can help address dilemmas between rights and health and safety concerns;
- support others in understanding and following safe practice.

This chapter covers:

Common Induction Standards – Standard 8 – Health and safety in an adult social care setting: Learning Outcome 2

Level 2 HSC 027 – Contribute to health and safety in health and social care: Learning Outcome 2

Level 3 HSC 037 – Promote and implement health and safety in health and social care: Learning Outcome 2

The importance of assessing health and safety risks in the work setting

You, your employer and others in the work setting all have an obligation to minimise risk and promote safe practice. Risk assessment makes safe practice more likely for the following reasons:

- The process will identify hazards and minimise the chances of harm.

- Training staff and, where appropriate, people with learning disabilities and carers, in risk assessment and providing information minimises the risks of accidents and other hazards.

- Risks can change over time so it is important to review assessments and amend as necessary so that they are appropriate to the current situation.

- Effective risk assessment provides better opportunities for people with learning disabilities to live their lives the way they want and make informed choices and decisions, with the necessary level of support. It can help you deal with the dilemma between an individual's rights and protecting him or her from harm. In cases where the person him or herself does not have the capacity to understand the risk, risk assessment can help the person's carer to make the relevant choices and decisions.

- Assessment of risk may indicate that changes would enhance health and safety and minimise risks. For example, working practices can be changed to make them safer or they can be updated or more appropriate equipment might minimise risks. The assessment might indicate the need for more relevant training.

- Assessment can make people more aware of risks and ways to avoid or minimise them.

- Involving people with learning disabilities in risk assessment can provide opportunities for them to understand risk, balance risks and benefits, make more informed choices and avoid or deal more effectively with adverse situations.

- Risk assessments can enable staff to bring to the employer's attention anything that may pose a risk, but has not previously been identified.

Your employer's legal responsibilities in relation to risk

Under the Health and Safety at Work Act 1974 and Management of Health and Safety at Work Regulations 1999, risk assessment is a legal requirement in work settings which employ more than five people. If a risk assessment shows that the work cannot be done safely, other arrangements have to be put in place. Risk assessment takes account of risks to employees, the person/s being supported, and anyone else involved.

The Health and Safety Executive in their document *Five Steps to Risk Assessment* describes a risk assessment as: '...simply a careful examination of what, in your work, could cause harm to people, so that you can weigh up whether you have taken enough precautions or should do more to prevent harm.'

There is no specific way of doing a risk assessment but the HSE suggests a five step approach:

1. Identify the hazards (remember, a hazard is anything that may cause harm).
2. Decide who might be harmed and how.
3. Evaluate the risks and decide on precautions.
4. Record your findings and implement them.
5. Review your assessment and update if necessary.

Your responsibilities

Under health and safety law you as an employee are required to:

*   follow the training you have received when using any work items your employer has given you;
*   take reasonable care of your own and other people's health and safety;
*   co-operate with your employer on health and safety;
*   tell someone (your employer, supervisor, or health and safety representative) if you think inadequate precautions are putting anyone's health and safety at serious risk (www.hse.gov.uk).

Risk assessment in an organisation

Here are some of the risk assessments commonly undertaken by health and social care organisations:

- Food safety and hygiene
- Moving and positioning/handling of people and objects
- Infection control
- Personal safety and lone working
- Fire safety
- How to deal with an emergency
- Smoking at work
- Use of hazardous (harmful) materials
- Waste management and disposal
- Security measures and visitors in the work setting

Risk assessment in someone's home

Risk assessment and control is also required when the work setting is someone's own home, but the approach is obviously less formal and written records are unlikely unless there are special circumstances (of offending behaviour, risk to life, etc.). In this instance the risk assessments will be an integral part of the support plan. Your employer, whether this is the person you support or a carer, or a support provider, must make sure that all measures are in place to minimise risks and provide you with any equipment necessary for you to do your job as required.

How and when to report potential health and safety risks

The degree of risk varies with the nature of an activity or event and the situation in which it occurs. For example:

Ruth and Ellen use a hoist when helping Martha with personal care. One day Martha slips through the sling and lands on the floor, though fortunately she slips out slowly and doesn't hurt herself. Should Ellen and Ruth report this?

It's pretty obvious, isn't it? Of course they should. Martha has been losing weight and becoming frailer so the sling that was once suitable could now put her in danger. Or perhaps they just didn't fasten it properly. Whatever the cause, it's an incident that needs to be reported. The risk needs to be re-assessed in relation to Martha's needs, by a moving and positioning specialist, and then control measures put into place.

You should report and/or seek advice on all situations which you consider present risks, verbally to your line manager or a designated health and safety representative and in writing according to the procedures of your organisation. If you identify health and safety risks in someone's home setting, these should be reported to your organisation or you should seek advice from a health and safety specialist if employed directly by the person you support, or a carer.

When to report risks you have identified

- When there is the danger of significant physical, sexual or psychological harm to someone you should report this immediately.

- When someone is putting him or herself at risk and does not seem to have the capacity to judge the harm that might result, you need to report this. For example when someone is staying out all night without telling people where she is going or someone is being coerced by friends to do something against his will.

- If an event occurs outside the work premises, report the risk as soon as you return.

- When safety control measures are inadequate or when additional measures are required, e.g. poor lighting is causing falls.

- When changes to work practices put people at risk, for example when new shift patterns mean residents are being left alone for long periods.

- When someone's abilities change and he or she can no longer manage something previously within their capability.

- When you suspect that someone might be ill, but they are unable to tell you – this is particularly relevant to people with profound and multiple learning disabilities.

You also have a responsibility to support other people in following safe practice. This includes your colleagues and the person/s you support, as well as any volunteers you work with. It can be tempting when time is short to ignore guidelines for safe practice, but to do so could cause harm to yourself and others, contravene your employer's procedures and even break the law.

Reporting risks that occur in someone's own home

In the same way as described above, you should make your employer aware of any risks which have not been included in the risk assessment. While you have a right to work in a safe environment, you must also recognise that you cannot expect some things to be changed in someone's own home, except in serious or dangerous situations.

Activity

Think about your own work setting and a person you support.

List three risks you are aware of in relation to supporting that person. These should preferably be risks you have identified yourself. If this is not possible, use ones which are part of existing risk assessments.

Next write beside each risk what you can do to minimise that risk.

Finally, state how and to whom you would report this risk if it has not been identified in risk assessments or who you would discuss it with for further information. What questions would you ask?

Involving people with a learning disability in risk assessment, choice and decision making

There is an increasing emphasis on the rights of people with learning disabilities to be involved in the assessment and management of their own risks and to take responsibility in doing so. This is supported and encouraged by the self advocacy movement and leading activists with learning disabilities. Obviously, the extent to which people do this relies on their capacity. Where the person him or herself is not able to manage their own risks, the responsibility can be taken by the prime carer.

Helen Sanderson and her colleagues argue that traditional methods of risk assessment are not appropriate for most people with a learning disability, and they advocate person centred approaches to risk assessment:

> Traditional methods of risk assessment are full of charts and scoring systems, but the person, their objectives, dreams and life seem to get lost somewhere

in the page of tick boxes and statistics… Person-centred planning approaches identify what is important to a person from his or her own perspective and find appropriate solutions. We commend person-centred approaches for everyone.

http:bit.ly/SDCWGk

You can find out more about this in the Department of Health's document *Independence, Choice and Risk: A Guide to Best Practice in Supported Decision Making* from www.dh.gov.uk

There is an increased emphasis on the rights of people with a learning disability to be involved in the assessment and management of their own risks.

A developing body of information is available for people employing their own support worker, much of which provides advice and guidance on risk assessment. You might like to follow up the references at the end of this chapter which provide further information about this area.

In your own work, you will be able to make use of your own knowledge of the person/s you support in deciding how you can best involve them (or their family members if more appropriate) in risk assessment.

Caroline goes regularly to the gym. She says:

'The staff at the gym know I'm blind and they help me on to and off the machines and make sure I'm safe. I use the treadmill, the cross trainer and the exercise bike. I'm fine as long as there's somebody with me. The same at swimming as long as there's somebody in the water with me.'

Caroline and her friends have discussed how important it is for staff also to have choice because if somebody doesn't like doing something – like the gym or swimming – it can spoil the activity and make the worker feel uncomfortable. Caroline says: 'So if possible, it's better to have a support worker with you who likes the activity and you can usually sort this out.'

Risk assessment and black and minority ethnic communities

Like all other aspects of service provision, risk assessment needs to be sensitive to culture, religion, ethnicity and gender. Risks which are deemed acceptable in one context may cause problems in another.

Research into risk and people from minority ethnic cultures is limited. What has been done has focused more on carers and service providers than people who use services. Risk assessment and procedures for dealing with risk are more likely to reflect the needs of black and minority ethnic communities if:

- there are more workers from black and minority ethnic communities;
- more is known and understood about religious and cultural needs in different communities;
- steps are taken to address assumptions and stereotypes;
- information is more accessible to black and minority ethnic communities – this isn't just about different languages but also culturally sensitive ways of working;
- the importance of religious and cultural identities is recognised.

(Taken from Community Care article on people with learning difficulties from BME backgrounds, http://bit.ly/UJAFa5)

How risk assessment can help address dilemmas between rights and health and safety concerns

Alaszewski et al. (1999) refer to this as the 'risk and empowerment' divide. In their research study on empowerment and protection, they looked at the development of policies and practices in risk assessment and management in services for adults with learning disabilities. They concluded that, if people with learning disabilities are to enjoy full lives in the community, organisations need to develop risk policies which embrace both protection and empowerment issues. A person centred approach to risk is ideally suited to support both of these notions, they say. (For more information on this study, go to www.understandingindividualneeds.com)

Changing philosophies, current thinking and greater awareness of equality and human rights have had a significant effect on the ways in which we provide support for people with a learning disability. This diversity of provision, together with our recognition that the people we support cannot and should not lead risk free lives, and should not be protected in ways that limit their freedom and choice, means that the range and type of risks they are exposed to may be greater than they were in the past. Risk is all too often given by services as a reason why people with a learning disability cannot do the things the rest of us do every day. Considerations about risk are further complicated by the fact that the person or group taking the decision is not always the person or group affected by the risk. (For more information on this, go to www. helensandersonassociates.co.uk)

The Department of Health (2007) makes the following points about risk, choice and decision making:

- Everyone perceives risk differently.

- Risk is often viewed negatively and can prevent people from doing things that most people take for granted.

- A perceived risk needs to be tested and assessed to see if it is real.

- Reasonable risk is about striking a balance between empowering people to make choices, while supporting them to take informed everyday risks.

- We need to recognise that making a choice can sometimes involve an element of risk.

- We have to help people understand their responsibilities and the implications of their choices, including any risks, as well as acknowledge that there will often be some risk, and that trying to remove it altogether can outweigh the quality of life benefits for the person.

> Balancing service user risk taking, rights, autonomy and empowerment with issues of protection in … a context of limited resources, increasing public scrutiny and fear of professional litigation is complex. (Mitchell and Glendinning, 2007)

So how can you deal with this balancing act and manage risk in a way that supports people's lifestyle choices while at the same time fulfilling your legal responsibilities and ensuring their health and safety?

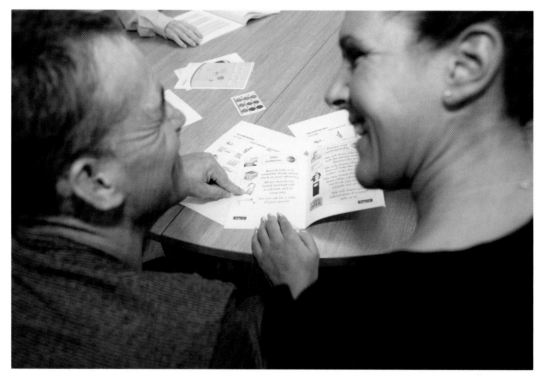

Using person centred approaches enables you to assess risk in the context of the person's rights, aspirations and capacity.

Using person centred approaches, as mentioned earlier in this chapter, enables you to assess risk in the context of the person's rights, aspirations and capacity. With your particular knowledge of the person/s you support, you will be in the best position to know how to do this, but you need to take account of the following:

- the capacity of the person to understand the risks involved, including the ability to weigh up the risk in relation to the gain;
- the level of risk involved for the person and others;
- his or her experience of risk taking and risk assessment;
- how you can explain the process and the potential risks in ways the individual understands;
- the extent to which the person's life will be limited if the risk is avoided;
- the safeguards that can be put in place to minimise the risk and to deal with any adverse consequences;
- the role, expectations and wishes of any family members involved with the person;
- positive versus negative consequences for the person.

Thinking point

'Individual adults who use social care and support services and/or their carers should be able to make their own decisions and take risks which they deem to be acceptable to lead their lives their way' (Close, 2009).

'Sometimes choices are so complex that people with learning disabilities find it very difficult to understand what is involved and this makes it difficult for them to make an informed choice. By 'informed choice' we mean that the person has assessed the implications and risks associated with that choice and still decided to make that choice' (Sellars, 2002).

Read these statements and think about them in relation to your own work? In the light of what you have read in this chapter, what do you have to take into account when thinking about risk in relation to the person or persons you support?

Key points from this chapter

- Risk is an essential part of life and can have positive as well as negative consequences.

- Under the Health and Safety at Work Act 1974 and Management of Health and Safety at Work Regulations 1999 your employer has to assess any risks associated with the work setting and work activities and put in place control measures.

- As a support worker you have a legal responsibility to cooperate with your employer in risk assessment and control, follow and promote safe working practices and report any additional risks you identify.

- Risk assessment can help you address dilemmas between rights and health and safety requirements by identifying and managing hazards, involving the person/s you support in identifying and managing risks and adopting a person centred approach to risk management and control.

References and where to go for more information

Alaszewski, H, Parker, A and Alaszewski, A (1999) *Empowerment and Protection: The development of policies and practices in risk assessment and risk management in services for adults with learning disabilities.* London: Mental Health Foundation

Alaszewski, H and Alaszewski, A (2005) 'Person-centred planning and risk: Challenging the boundaries' in Cambridge, P and Carnaby, S (eds.) *Person-centred Planning and Care Management with People with Learning Disabilities.* London: Jessica Kingsley Publishers, pp.183–97

Close, L (2009) *Safeguarding and Personalisation: Two Sides of the Same Coin.* www.shop4support.com

Community Care (2005) *People with Learning Disabilities from BME Backgrounds.* www.communitycare.co.uk

Department of Health (DH) (2007) *Independence, Choice and Risk: A Guide to Best Practice in Supported Decision Making.* www.dh.gov.uk

Health and Safety Executive (HSE) (2011) *Five Steps to Risk Assessment* www.hse.gov.uk

Health and Safety Executive (HSE) (2009) *Health and Safety Law: What you Need to Know.* www.hse.gov.uk

Healthy Working Lives (2012) *Management of Health and Safety at Work Regulations 1999.* www.healthyworkinglives.com

Helen Sanderson Associates (2012) *Person Centred Risk.* www.helensandersonassociates.co.uk

Mitchell, W and Glendinning, C (2007) *Risk and Adult Social Care: What Does UK Research Evidence Tell Us?* Paper presented at 'Risk and Rationalities Conference', organised by the ESRC Social Contexts and Responses Risk Network. www.kent.ac.uk

Sellars, C (2002) 'Assessment of risk in people with learning disabilities: why is it needed?', in *Risk Assessment in People with Learning Disabilities.* Oxford: BPS Blackwell.

Social Care Institute for Excellence (SCIE) (2010) *Report 36: Enabling Risk, Ensuring Safety: Self-directed Support and Personal Budgets.* www.scie.org.uk

Tilley, L (2011) *Person Centred Approaches when Supporting People with a Learning Disability.* Exeter: BILD/Learning Matters

Understanding Individual Needs.com (2012) *Care and Support Services – Safeguarding Standards. Considering Risk.* www.understandingindividualneeds.com

Chapter 3

Responding to accidents and sudden illness

Dave is a keen athlete and spends a lot of time training. One day at the track he loses his footing and lands awkwardly with one leg twisted under him. It seems likely he has broken his leg so he is taken to the accident and emergency department of his local hospital. Shakeel his support worker goes with him. Accident reports are needed at the sports centre and at the day centre Dave attends.

Introduction

In this chapter you are asked to think about your own responsibilities in responding to any accidents or sudden illness that might occur in your own work setting. Responding calmly and effectively in such situations is the key to getting the right help as quickly as possible, preventing further injury and even saving someone's life.

Learning outcomes

This chapter will help you to:

- describe the different types of accident and sudden illness that may occur in your own work setting;
- explain the procedures to be followed if an accident or sudden illness should occur;
- be aware of tasks relating to emergency first aid that you are not allowed to carry out at your current stage of training.

This chapter covers:

Common Induction Standards – Standard 8 – Health and safety in an adult social care setting: Learning Outcome 4

Level 2 HSC 027 – Contribute to health and safety in health and social care: Learning Outcome 3

Level 3 HSC 037 – Promote and implement health and safety in health and social care: Learning Outcome 3

The types of accidents or sudden illness that might occur in your work setting

Many of the accidents and illnesses that occur in your work setting are likely to be fairly minor such as bumps or grazes, small cuts or bruises, or illnesses such as colds and flu. Most people with learning disabilities are no more prone to accidents and sudden illness than the rest of us, but some are, especially those with more complex health needs. People whose behaviour challenges services may also be more at risk from accidents to themselves or others, especially if it's difficult for them to understand the consequences of their actions.

You need to be prepared in case you have to deal with more serious incidents, such as:

- an injury that results from a fall (falls are the most common cause of injury in residential care homes), such as a bump on the head, a fracture or suspected fracture;

- burns and scalds;

- severe bleeding;

- an epileptic seizure;

- choking or other difficulties with breathing, such as those caused by asthma or cardiac arrest;

- electric shock;

- serious injuries to eyes;

- fevers and very high temperatures;

- unconsciousness;

- prolonged vomiting.

You need to know:

- the procedures to be followed if an accident or sudden illness occurs in your work setting;
- what you can safely do at your current stage of training;
- what to include when you are recording and reporting the incident for your employer.

Thinking point

Think about the kind of work you do. Are you always in the same building or do you use different venues? Do you work outside and inside? Do you use equipment?

Which of the places you work in and which of the activities you're involved in are most likely to give rise to accidents? What do you do to avoid these accidents?

The policies and procedures of your work setting in relation to accidents and sudden illness

In organisations

Policies and procedures should provide clear guidelines for employees and others such as:

- how to keep safe in the area where the incident occurs;
- how to keep the person/s from further injury;
- how to summon emergency help and who to summon;
- who the trained first aiders or appointed persons are in the work setting;
- how to report the accident or illness.

Employers are also required to have:

- an appointed person who can take charge in an emergency;
- a suitably equipped first aid box;
- a notice saying where the first aid box is and who the appointed person is;
- trained first aiders and, if the workplace gives rise to special hazards, a first aid room;
- information that takes account of different language needs.

As an employee you must make sure you are familiar with the procedures to be followed if an accident or sudden illness does occur when you are working, whether it involves you, someone you support or another person.

In someone's own home

If you are employed directly by the person you support, or a family member, you should agree with the person procedures to be followed in the event of an accident or sudden illness. These might include:

- particular risks or health issues which could result in emergencies, for example diabetes, epilepsy, heart conditions, asthma, impaired mobility, etc.;

- the types of emergency that might occur;

- what to do in the event of an emergency;

- named people to contact and how to access emergency phone numbers;

- how to keep the person safe, secure and how to provide reassurance.

If you work in someone's home, but are employed by a support provider, the points above will still apply and will have been discussed with the person and/ or family member as part of the support plan. Your employer will also have policies and procedures that have to be followed, including how to report the accident or illness.

In an organisation or someone's home you should draw to your manager's attention and/or report any hazards that could cause accidents. Things like torn rugs, frayed electrical cords, large obstacles, broken handles, hot taps that don't turn off properly, burned out light bulbs, chipped crockery, broken plant pots, trailing flexes, overloaded sockets and wet floors are the kinds of things that can go unreported but which can cause serious accidents.

You should report any hazards that could cause an accident.

If you are employed by an organisation, read through your employer's policies and procedures for responding to accidents and sudden illness.

If you are employed by the person you support or a family carer, look at the relevant section of the person's support plan or your contract of employment and discuss agreed procedures with the person concerned.

Now answer the following questions, basing your answers on what you have just read or discussed.

- *In the event of an accident or sudden illness in your work setting, what should you do to make the area and the person safe?*
- *Which kind of emergency service or support will you call for?*
- *How will you report the incident and to whom?*
- *What other steps do you have to take?*

If you are unable to answer any of these questions discuss them with your line manager or person employing you.

What you can and cannot do at your current stage of training

It is extremely important that you know what your current training permits you to do in the event of an accident or sudden illness so that you do not cause any further harm. If you work for an organisation and an accident happens and you are not appropriately trained you should seek help immediately from a qualified first aider. Make sure you know which of your colleagues have already completed their first aid course and who the named first aiders are in your work place. If you work in someone's house, you should discuss first aid training with the person who employs you and get further advice from people with the appropriate expertise – this could be from the local authority or from the organisation which employs you.

If you have not yet been trained in first aid you should:

- summon help as quickly as you can;

- assist the qualified first aider or health professional who attends the situation, following all instructions as given;

- keep yourself and other people safe, by removing any hazards which might cause additional problems to the casualty, yourself or other people but only if it is safe to do so;

- help to clear people from the scene to save any further problems and protect the casualty's dignity;

- help those who may have witnessed the accident or illness who might be distressed.

Recording and reporting accidents and sudden illnesses

Recording and reporting accidents and sudden illnesses is important for a number of reasons, including:

- to ensure that there is an accurate record of what happened;

- to learn from the incident and see if there are ways of preventing its recurrence;

- to comply with legal obligations.

If you work in an organisation you have a responsibility to report accidents and sudden illnesses to your employer in the way specified in health and safety procedures. This will include:

- the date and time of the accident or illness;

- details of the casualty and others present;

- details of how the accident or illness occurred;

- the injury sustained or relevant details of the illness;

- any other relevant details.

Thinking point

Are you clear about the reporting procedure for accidents and illnesses in your own work setting including who to report to, how to report and how to make a record of the incident?

Organisations and agencies will have a prescribed procedure for accident reporting. Your employer, if an organisation, has legal obligations under the Reporting of Injuries, Diseases and Dangerous Occurrences Regulations 1995 (RIDDOR).

Under RIDDOR and best practice guidelines, accidents and sudden illnesses should be reported so that there is an accurate record with as much detail as possible and in order to prevent similar incidents.

RIDDOR also requires that employers must report:

- deaths;
- major injuries;
- accidents resulting in more than seven days off work;
- diseases contracted at work or through workplace activities;
- dangerous occurrences, such as failure of lifting equipment, burst pipes, or electrical short circuits that cause fire or explosion.

If your organisation is subject to regulation and inspection, these should also be reported to the relevant regulating body.

Reportable injuries	Reportable diseases
Fracture other than to fingers, thumbs or toes	Certain poisonings
Amputation	
Dislocation of the shoulder, hip, knee or spine	Some skin diseases, e.g. occupational dermatitis, skin cancer, chrome ulcer, oil folliculitis acne
Loss of sight (temporary or permanent)	
Chemical or hot metal burn to the eye or any penetrating injury to the eye	Lung diseases, e.g. occupational asthma, farmer's lung, pneumoconiosis, asbestosis, mesothelioma
Injury resulting from an electric shock or electrical burn leading to unconsciousness or requiring resuscitation or admittance to hospital for more than 24 hours	
Any other injury which leads to hypothermia (getting too cold), heat-induced illness or unconsciousness; requires resuscitation; or requires admittance to hospital for more than 24 hours	Infections, e.g. leptospirosis, hepatitis, tuberculosis, anthrax, legionelliosis (Legionnaries' disease) and tetanus
Unconsciousness caused by asphyxia (suffocation) or exposure to a harmful substance or biological agent	
Acute illness requiring medical treatment or leading to a loss of consciousness, arising from absorption of any substance by inhalation, ingestion or through the skin	Other conditions, e.g. occupational cancer, certain musculoskeletal disorders, decompression illness and hand-arm vibration syndrome
Acute illness requiring medical treatment where there is reason to believe that this resulted from exposure to a biological agent or its toxins or infected material	

You also have responsibilities in relation to RIDDOR, which involve:

- knowing your organisation's policies and procedures;
- knowing where to access accident reporting forms and when and how to use them;
- reporting any accidents, illnesses or dangerous occurrences in accordance with the policies and procedures;
- completing a report following any incident, as required by your employer.

Another piece of legislation that applies to emergency situations is the Health and Safety (First-Aid) Regulations 1981, which identifies the three main aims of first aid as follows:

1. To preserve life until a doctor, nurse or paramedic arrives.
2. To minimise the consequences of the injury or illness until help arrives.
3. To treat minor injuries that do not require treatment by a doctor, nurse or paramedic.

Employers must assess the level of first aid provision needed. Formal written recording is not required but is recommended. Quick responses and initial management of injury and illness at work can save lives and prevent minor injuries becoming more serious.

You can find out more about completing reports and records in the book in this series, *Handling Information for a Learning Disability Worker* (2011) by Lesley Barcham and Jackie Pountney.

Basic emergency techniques

This section outlines some basic emergency techniques. This is only for information and does not replace first aid training. **You should not undertake any first aid procedures unless you have been trained**. Remember that to be either a first aider or an appointed person you must attend an approved training course. If you have already undertaken first aid training and been assessed as competent, you need to be clear about what you can and cannot do at your current stage of training. In all of the situations described it is vital to summon medical help immediately.

Thinking point

If you have not had first aid training, have you discussed with your line manager or a senior colleague what you should do if you have to respond to an accident or sudden illness? Are you clear about the organisation's policy and procedures and how they apply to you?

If employed directly by someone with a learning disability, or their relative, have you discussed with them the procedures outlined in the person's support plan or in your agreed ways of working?

If you have had first aid training, are you fully aware of what you can and cannot do at your stage of training? If not, discuss this with someone who can advise you.

Problems with breathing

There may be a variety of reasons why someone isn't breathing, for example something such as food or vomit could be blocking the airway.

ABC (airway–breathing–circulation) is the procedure used to assess someone's breathing and to help ensure that oxygen is supplied to the brain and vital organs while waiting for help to arrive. If the airway is blocked the person will be unable to breathe and oxygen will not reach the brain or other vital organs, resulting in death or disability. Different guidance is given on resuscitation procedures for babies, children and adults and the number of breaths and compressions needed to ensure an effective supply of oxygen. It is therefore vital that you get proper first aid training before attempting this procedure.

The ABC procedure has three steps:

- Airway
- Breathing
- Circulation

The starting point is to check that the airway is clear. This can be done in a number of ways:

- Check by looking and listening to see if the person is breathing.
- Try shaking the person and calling their name to see if they respond.
- Tilt the head back by using your first and middle finger and check in the mouth to see if a piece of food or other object is lodged at the back of the throat. If there is, you will need to follow the procedure for choking later in this section.

- If there are no signs of obstruction, ensure that the airway is fully open, then pinch the nose between the thumb and forefinger of one hand while using the other hand to press on the chin to open the casualty's mouth.

- Make sure that you have a secure 'seal' around the mouth, so that air cannot escape, and then blow into the mouth twice. If any colleagues are present shout for them to ring the ambulance.

- If there is no one else around blow into the mouth ten times then as quickly as possible ring for an ambulance.

- Once help has been called continue giving two rescue breaths, then check whether the person is breathing, then two rescue breaths and so on until the ambulance arrives or the person begins to breathe on their own.

This action could be enough to keep a person alive until they can breathe for themselves.

Pinch the nose between the thumb and forefinger of one hand while using the other hand to press on the chin to open the casualty's mouth.

Choking

Choking is usually the body's response to an object being lodged at the back of the throat. A quick response is vital so that the person doesn't stop breathing.

- If the person wears false teeth or dentures, make sure you remove these first.

- Sweep the mouth with a gloved finger to clear the food, vomit or obstruction from the throat.

- Ask the person to cough if at all possible. If this is not effective move on to the next step.

- Bend the person forwards. Slap them sharply on the back between the shoulder blades five times.

- If this fails, use the Heimlich manoeuvre, but only if you have been trained to do so. Stand behind the person with your arms around them. Join your hands together in a fist, just under the sternum (breastbone).

- Sharply pull your joined hands upwards and into the person's body at the same time. This should free the obstruction.

- At this point an ambulance should be called. If the obstruction hasn't been cleared it will need someone qualified to help remove it. If it has been removed, the ambulance will still need to be called to check the casualty hasn't sustained any injuries from the Heimlich manoeuvre.

- You should alternate backslaps and abdominal thrusts until either the obstruction is cleared or the ambulance arrives.

Only use the Heimlich manoeuvre if you have been trained to do so.

Dysphagia

Dysphagia – difficulties with eating, drinking or swallowing – is a serious problem for some people with a learning disability, especially those who have additional health needs or profound and multiple learning disabilities. The safe and proper management of dysphagia can prevent choking and reduce risks to life.

The National Patient Safety Agency provides guidance on best practice for the management of dysphagia. This includes:

- services for people with learning disabilities having policies in place dealing specifically with dysphagia;

- ensuring that anyone with dysphagia has an individualised plan with guidelines for managing their dysphagia; this should include an eating, drinking and swallowing care plan;

- the accurate reporting of all incidents involving dysphagia;

- accessible information on dysphagia management, including advice on the preparation of suitable foods and fluids;

- individual risk assessments for everyone with dysphagia;

- the support and advice of a suitably qualified professional, i.e. a speech and language therapist or specialist practitioner.

(NHS, 2007, *Ensuring Safer Practice for Adults with Learning Disabilities who have Dysphagia*, www.nrls.npsa.nhs.uk)

The most appropriate people to provide advice about dysphagia and related problems are speech and language therapists. All services for people with a learning disability should have access to such therapists through a GP referral. Regular support from a speech and language therapist is particularly important for services which provide support for people with additional health needs or profound and multiple learning disabilities.

Loss of consciousness

Loss of consciousness can happen for several reasons, such as fainting, an epileptic seizure, a bang on the head, etc. The person is unresponsive or has a much reduced level of awareness and responsiveness.

The recovery position is used for casualties who are unconscious, to ensure that the airway is maintained (kept clear), that vomit is not inhaled and that the person is in a safe position until help arrives. However, if you suspect that someone has a back or neck injury and possibly a fracture of any part of the body it is advisable not to use this procedure as you may make their condition worse.

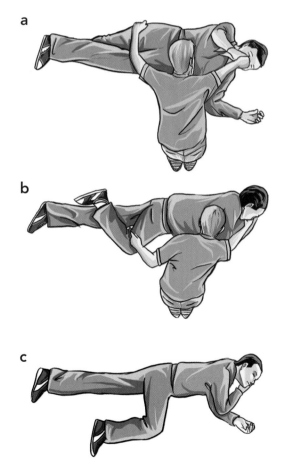

To put a person in the recovery position you should follow these steps:

- Kneel at the side of the casualty at about waist level.

- Tilt back the person's head – this will open the airway. The casualty should be laid on their back with their arms and legs straight.

- Bend the arm closest to you at the elbow, at right angles to the body, as if they are waving.

- Pull the arm which is on the opposite side to you across the casualty's chest, placing the back of the casualty's hand on their opposite cheek (see diagram a).

The recovery position.

- Roll the casualty towards you by pulling on the leg furthest away from you, just above the knee (see diagram b). The casualty should now be on their side.

- Once the casualty is on their side, bend the leg at right angles to the body and tilt the head well back to ensure the airway is kept open (see diagram c).

Epilepsy

As a support worker you may have to respond in a situation in which someone you support has an epileptic seizure, so it is important to be clear about what to do. As with everything else, you should only act in accordance with the level of training you have received.

Epilepsy is a neurological condition in which an individual has seizures which start in the brain. There are different types of epileptic seizures and seizures can be different for each person. Most seizures happen suddenly, last for a short time and stop by themselves. Not all seizures are convulsive (jerking or shaking). It is particularly important for you to know how to react when someone has a convulsive seizure. When someone has an epileptic seizure you should take the following steps:

- Stay calm.

- Look around to see if the person is in a dangerous place. If not, don't move them, but move anything that might cause them harm and that can be moved, such as furniture.

- Note the time the seizure starts so that you will know how long it lasts and can keep checking the time.

- Stay with the person.

- Cushion the person's head with something soft.

- Don't hold the person down or put anything in their mouth.

- Check the time again. **If the convulsive seizure doesn't stop after five minutes, or if the person has stopped breathing, call an ambulance**.

- After the seizure, put the person in the recovery position (as described above) and check that their breathing has returned to normal.

- Stay with the person until they have returned to normal.

- **If the person has another seizure without recovering fully from the first seizure, call an ambulance.**

For more information go to www.epilepsysociety.org.uk

If the person you support is at risk from choking or loss of breath because of seizures, or something else, a risk assessment and preventative measures should be part of their support plan, e.g. how their food should be prepared (blended, for instance), how they should be fed or assisted to feed themselves, how medication should be given (liquid instead of pills, for example). This helps minimise the risk. There should also be guidance on what to do if the person requires first aid.

Cardiac arrest

Cardiac arrest means that the heart has stopped beating. It can happen as a result of a heart attack, electric shock or for other reasons. Medical help must be summoned urgently. The person will have no pulse and will have stopped breathing.

The response to cardiac arrest is cardiopulmonary resuscitation (CPR). This involves mouth to mouth resuscitation to provide oxygen and chest compression to stimulate the heart. **You can only give CPR if you have attended a special course where you will learn the techniques and apply them under supervision**. Your responsibility if you have not attended such a course is to get medical help immediately.

Severe bleeding

Most bleeding that you come across as a support worker will be from relatively minor cuts. These will require minimal first aid, such as cleaning the wound and dressing it. Outlined below is the technique involved when the casualty has sustained an injury which results in more severe bleeding. Severe bleeding means large amounts of blood from the wound.

Severe bleeding will require urgent medical attention, so an ambulance must be called for immediately as loss of blood could result in shock or loss of consciousness. Make sure that you take the necessary precautions to protect yourself throughout this technique.

- Pressure should be applied directly to the wound for at least ten minutes to allow the blood to clot. Use a sterile dressing to do this or any other absorbent material that is available.

- If there is an object in the wound, such as glass, do not remove it. Apply pressure to the sides of the wound.

- Lay the person down and raise the affected part.
- Make the person comfortable and secure until help arrives.

Always wear protective gloves and wash your hands before and after carrying out any of these techniques.

Suspected fractures

The symptoms of a fracture can include the following: severe pain, swelling, discolouration, the affected limb or joint in an unnatural position, bone protruding through the skin.

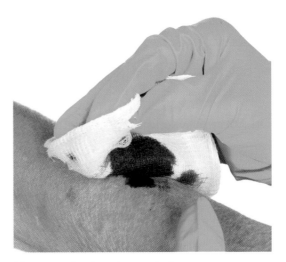

Use a sterile dressing and always wear protective gloves.

If you suspect that someone has broken or cracked a bone, it is important to get the person to hospital as soon as possible so that a correct diagnosis is made and the appropriate medical treatment given.

- Make sure the person is comfortable, and ensure they remain as still as possible.
- Provide reassurance.
- Unless it is absolutely necessary, i.e. there is immediate danger, do not move the person.
- Support the injured limb using your hands, clothing, towels, etc.
- Do not try to bandage or splint a fracture yourself.

Burns and scalds

Burns and scalds range from minor, such as a small burn on a finger, to severe and life threatening, such as someone getting into a bath of scalding water, or burns from electrical equipment or chemicals. The skin is red, tender and there may be swelling, especially with severe burns.

Immediate help should be sought for severe burns and burns covering a large area. You should follow these steps:

- Make sure the person is safe from further burns.
- Remove the source of heat if still a danger and if it is possible to do this without danger to you and the person involved.

- Cool the affected area with cool water (preferably running) for 20 minutes if possible.

- Follow any advice given by the person attending or dealing with the burn or scald.

Do not remove clothing or anything else stuck to the burn, touch or cover a burn or apply anything to the burn, such as ointment.

Key points from this chapter

It's important for you to be aware of the kinds of accidents and sudden illnesses that might occur in your particular work setting and of the circumstances that might give rise to them, by:

- making sure you are familiar with the risk assessments for the different activities people engage in;

- knowing how to deal with any incidents arising because of particular conditions – for example epilepsy or diabetes;

- being aware of and reporting any hazards you identify that might cause accidents.

As a support worker you have a responsibility to follow your employer's policies and procedures for responding to accidents and sudden illness. This includes knowing:

- how to summon help and who to call on;

- how to support the person and assist a first aider;

- how to record and report accidents and sudden illness;

- what you can and cannot do at your current stage of training.

References and where to go for more information

References

Barcham, L and Pountney, J (2011) *Handling Information for a Learning Disability Worker.* Exeter: Learning Matters/BILD

British Red Cross (2012) *Everyday First Aid.* www.redcross.org.uk

Health and Safety Executive (HSE) (2009) *Health and Safety (First-Aid) Regulations 1981 Approved Code of Practice and Guidance.* www.hse.gov.uk

Health and Safety Executive (HSE) (2012) *Reporting of Injuries, Diseases and Dangerous Occurrences Regulations 1995 (RIDDOR).* www.hse.gov.uk

NHS (2007) *Ensuring Safer Practice for Adults with Learning Disabilities who have Dysphagia.* www.nrls.npsa.nhs.uk

Websites

The Epilepsy Society www.epilepsysociety.org.uk

Christine has cerebral palsy and uses an electric wheelchair. A few years ago she was diagnosed with lymphoedema for which she has to wear compression stockings and use compression bandages. She and one of her support workers, Cheryl, went to the local hospital and were shown how to put the stockings on and apply the bandages, while taking care not to damage Christine's skin which is very fragile. Breaks in her skin could result in serious complications to her health. Christine and Cheryl then trained the second support worker. Christine also discussed with all three the importance of avoiding knocks to her skin to avoid bleeding or other damage. The procedures they have worked out are reviewed regularly to make sure they are working.

Introduction

Being dependent on other people for your personal care, as Christine is, means that you have to trust them and be sure that they work *with* you rather than *for* you and carry out care tasks with sensitivity – in other words, that care is person centred and not task orientated. Workers also need to know what they're doing and have special training in order to work safely and avoid doing harm. This is particularly important in relation to medication and health care tasks.

Learning outcomes

This chapter will help you to:

- understand the main points of agreed ways of working about medication agreed with your employer;

- understand the main points of agreed ways of working about health care tasks agreed with your employer;

- be aware of tasks relating to medication and health care procedures which you are not allowed to carry out at your current stage of training.

'Agreed ways of working' covers policy and procedures in organisations as well as work procedures in someone's home.

This chapter covers:

Common Induction Standards – Standard 8 – Health and safety in an adult social care setting: Learning Outcome 5

Legislation

The main legislation regulating the administration and storage of medication includes:

- The Medicines Act 1968
- The Misuse of Drugs Act 1971
- The Misuse of Drugs (Safe Custody) Regulations 1973
- The Misuse of Drugs (Amendment No 2) (England, Wales and Scotland) Regulations 2012
- Guidelines from the Royal Pharmaceutical Society of Great Britain

The Medicines and Healthcare Products Regulatory Agency (MHRA) Enforcement & Intelligence Group (E & I) has responsibility for enforcing medicines legislation in England and does so in Scotland and Wales on behalf of the Scottish Parliament and the Welsh Assembly. In Northern Ireland the Medicines Regulatory Group is responsible for medicines control.

You don't need to know the details of the legislation, but you do need to follow the procedures set out by your employer and/or agreed ways of working if you support someone in their own home, all of which must comply with the legislation.

In an organisation, policies and procedures relating to medication and health care will include specific instructions for:

- ordering and receiving medication;
- storing medication safely;

- giving medication or assisting someone who manages their own medication;

- carrying out specialised health care tasks;

- keeping records;

- disposing of medication;

- providing information to the people taking the medication;

- dealing with any problems arising from the use or consequences of medication.

In some settings, such as nursing homes and some residential homes, registered nursing staff will have primary responsibility for medication and health care tasks. There may also be other health professionals who undertake specific tasks, such as podiatrists, who will deal with specialised foot care, and district nurses, who may give injections and change catheters or dressings.

If your work takes place in someone's own home and you are employed by the person you support, or their family carer, any medication and health care tasks the person requires will be written into their care assessment and support plan. If you are required to assist them you will be trained to do so. Community health professionals such as district nurses, continence advisers, podiatrists or moving and handling specialists might be involved in the person's health care.

Your responsibilities in relation to medication and health care in your work setting

Your role in giving or assisting with medication and undertaking health tasks will depend on:

- how long you have been a support worker;

- the level of training you have received;

- the type of setting you work in.

You are not permitted to assist in giving medication or in undertaking health care tasks until you have received the appropriate training. Medication must only be managed by people who have been specially trained in order to:

- ensure the safety of the person taking it and, where relevant, other people, i.e. to see that it is given and taken correctly;

- comply with legislation;

- ensure accountability.

Depending on where you work, training will be provided by your employer, the local authority, a specialist agency, or perhaps by a district nurse. In an organisation, your induction will include an introduction to policies and procedures on medication and health care. At this stage your role will be that of an observer.

Once you have been trained and signed off as competent for any medical procedure, you must always follow the risk assessment and support plan for the person involved. You also need to keep records as agreed and note any changes or incidents. If you are unsure about anything you must always seek help. Errors with medication and health care tasks can be serious or even fatal.

The points above apply to both prescribed medication and 'over-the-counter' medicines such as pain killers, cough remedies, pain relieving gels or lotions and other readily available medicines.

In relation to shop bought (over-the-counter) medication, there must be clear guidance in the person's care or support plan about *what* you are authorised to do, *how* and *when* you are permitted to administer such medication, the *correct dosage* and any additional relevant guidance. If you are unsure about any aspect of shop bought medication you *must* seek guidance from your line manager or the appropriate health professional, just as you would for prescribed medication.

Principles relating to the safe handling of medicines

The Royal Pharmaceutical Society provides guidelines for the safe handling of medicines in social care settings (*The Handling of Medicines in Social Care* is available at: www.rpharms.com). **This is provided as background information only and does not replace training to give or otherwise manage medication. You must do a recognised course and be assessed as competent in order to handle medication or undertake health care tasks in the UK**.

The legislation governing medication and social care providers differs in England, Wales, Scotland and Northern Ireland. Your employer or local council will be able to provide you with information for your part of the UK.

The Royal Pharmaceutical Society has identified a set of principles relating to the safe and appropriate handling of medicines. These apply to every social care organisation. The society provides guidance on how these principles apply in practice in health and social care settings. For example:

- People have a right to choice, e.g. as to the pharmacy which provides their medication, looking after their own medicines, taking their own medication with help from staff, consent in relation to medication and so on.
- People must be included in decisions about their own treatment, e.g. having a flu jab.
- The person's dignity and privacy must be respected and preserved.
- Support workers are not allowed to give medication unless they have been appropriately trained and assessed as competent.
- Organisations must have written procedures that set out exactly how to give medicines and it is good practice to monitor workers to see that they follow these procedures.
- Written procedures for giving medicines should be simple and easy to follow. Once trained and judged competent to give certain medicines, you should be familiar with this procedure and follow it carefully.
- People should receive the right medicines at the right time and in the right way.
- Medicines should be stored safely and in the right way, e.g. not in heat or dampness.
- Unwanted medicines should be disposed of safely.
- Medicines should only be given to the person they are prescribed for.
- Where support workers work in a person's home they may need to clarify who will be responsible for requesting repeat prescriptions – the person or a relative – unless this forms part of the care package.
- Whenever possible people in care settings should be responsible for looking after and taking their own medicines, but this will not always be possible.
- Some medicines have to be taken at particular times, such as before, with or after food (the absence or presence of food in the stomach can affect how the medicine works and may cause unwanted effects).
- Some illnesses can only be controlled with very precise dose timings, e.g. some people's seizures are only controlled if they take their tablets at set times.

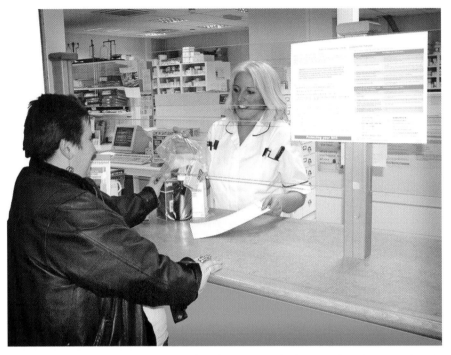

People have a right to choice, e.g. as to the pharmacy which provides their medication.

Some of these points will apply to all support settings, but some will be more relevant to organisations rather than support in someone's home. The extent to which the person you support will be able to manage their own medication will depend on their capacity to understand and other things, such as whether they have additional physical impairment which limits movement or causes particular difficulty, for example with swallowing.

The results of administering medication incorrectly can be catastrophic and as a consequence it is seen as a protection of vulnerable adults (POVA) issue which may result in an allegation of abuse being made. So it is very important to make sure you are clear about what your role and responsibilities are to ensure that both the person you support and you are kept safe.

Once you are trained, your role might be to assist qualified health care professionals. This could include:

- monitoring a person's condition and making records;
- supporting the person to do as much as possible themselves in relation to other health care needs;
- undertaking tasks you have been trained to do such as applying creams or changing dressings.

Think of someone you assist in taking their medication or who you will assist once you have been trained. Check that you are clear about the following points, then discuss your answers with your line manager:

- *What is the medication for (unless there is a particular reason why this is confidential)?*
- *Why does the person need assistance?*
- *What form does the medication take, e.g. pills, cream, injection?*
- *If there is anything you are not clear about, who will you ask for information?*

Health care tasks

Many of the points above in relation to medication also apply to any health care tasks you might have to undertake. As with medication, **you are not allowed to undertake health care tasks until you have been trained and judged competent to carry out those particular tasks**.

Health care tasks include such things as:

- changing or helping someone to change stoma bags (colostomy, ileostomy);
- giving injections, e.g. insulin for diabetes;
- giving drugs rectally, e.g. suppositories, diazepam (for epileptic seizure);
- giving oxygen.

If you work in an organisation and have any concerns about any health care tasks you are asked to undertake you should reread the policies and procedures and check things out with your line manager. You need to be sure about the limit of your responsibility, who to ask if you are unsure about anything you do, what to do if a mistake is made and what training you should have before taking on the tasks. If you are employed by the person you support or a carer, you can get information and advice from the person but if you are unsure about anything you should discuss this and seek further assistance from a doctor, district nurse or relevant health professional.

Many of the intimate care tasks you undertake have implications for the person's health, e.g. stoma care, changing continence pads, emptying catheter bags. You should be trained how to do all relevant health care tasks and the information, including a risk assessment, should be provided in the person's support plan. If you work in an organisation, the information should be provided in health care policies and procedures.

When undertaking any health care tasks or providing support relating to personal and intimate care you should also remember the key values of person-centred support and maintaining the person's dignity in everything you do. This includes:

- spending time getting to know the person before undertaking any of these tasks;

- seeking consent for what you are doing;

- explaining what you are doing and checking that the person is all right throughout;

- following what is set out in the support plan or health action plan to be sure you provide support in the way the person prefers;

- following good practice, which includes providing personal and intimate care for a person of the same sex as yourself, for example women with women.

In the case of both health care tasks and personal and intimate care, it is crucial that tasks are done in line with policies, procedures and support plans, risk assessments or health action plans. Anything which is done that is not covered by these, or isn't done and should be, could leave the person in a potentially risky situation. This could pose a threat to their health, safety and well-being and could result in consequences for you as the support worker no matter how good your intentions.

Medication and health care procedures which you are not allowed to carry out at your current stage of training

It is important that you are clear about what you can and cannot do at each stage of your training. You are only allowed to give medicines that you have been trained to give and undertake health tasks for which you have had special training. In both instances you have to be observed and assessed as competent. Once trained, you might be involved in giving certain kinds of medication, supervising someone who self medicates, using creams or ointments, eye or ear drops.

Spend time getting to know the person before undertaking any healthcare tasks.

You will only be able to undertake the following tasks if you have had additional training and been judged competent to carry out these tasks:

- Rectal drug administration, e.g. suppositories, diazepam (for epileptic seizure).

- Giving injectable drugs such as insulin.

- Administering medication through a Percutaneous Endoscopic Gastrostomy (PEG).

- Giving oxygen.

If you have been trained and assessed as competent to administer rectal diazepam for epileptic seizures, there may be occasions when it is not possible to do this, e.g. when you are in a public setting and the person's privacy and dignity would be compromised. It is necessary therefore, to have an alternative approach in place for such situations. Detailed information about this must be clearly stated in the person's care plan.

Services for people with a learning disability must be aware of the policy of their local social and health services in relation to the administration of rectal diazepam and ensure that their employees are informed about these. If you are unsure about any aspect of these policies and what you are and are not allowed to do you must seek advice from your line manager, if employed by an organisation, or the relevant health professional (GP or district nurse, for instance) if employed by the person you support or a family carer.

If you know or suspect that there have been any errors with medication:

- You must report this immediately to your line manager and follow directions given.

- Your line manager or other appropriate person must report immediately to the prescriber/GP/pharmacist and follow directions given.

If a serious error is made the person may need hospital treatment. Any error must be fully documented. All incidents should be fully investigated, the results documented and every possible action taken to prevent the mistake happening again. You can find out more in *Medication Administration in Social Care*, available at www.socialcareassociation.co.uk

Activity

If you work in an organisation

Make a list of the medicines you know are administered in your service and what they are for. Do the same with health care tasks.

Now describe how you would give or assist with giving one of these medicines to, or undertaking a health care task with, someone in a person centred way while following your organisation's procedures. Take into account:

- *whether the person self administers (takes medication him or herself) with supervision or has to be given the medication;*
- *how much support the person needs;*
- *how you would communicate to explain, reassure, ask questions, etc.;*
- *why it's important to follow your organisation's procedures;*
- *why it's important to work in a person centred way when giving or assisting with medication or undertaking or assisting with health care tasks.*

If you work in someone's own home

Discuss with the person you support, and/or a carer, if appropriate, any medication he or she takes and health care tasks you are required to assist with and agreed ways of working. Include in your discussion:

▶

- *the person's own requirements in how these should be managed;*
- *what he or she requires from you;*
- *why it's important to be clear about your role;*
- *who you could approach if you need any more information.*

When you have finished this task talk to your line manager about your findings.

Key points from this chapter

- The administration and storage of medication is strictly controlled by law. The main piece of legislation is the Medicines Act 1968.

- You need to be trained and assessed as competent in order to give medication or undertake health care tasks and to be aware of what you can and cannot do at your current stage of training.

- Training is required to comply with legal requirements, safeguard people and ensure that people are accountable for their actions.

- You must know and adhere to your employer's policies and procedures or agreed ways of working in relation to medication and health care tasks. This includes procedures for ordering, storing, administering and disposing of medication.

References and where to go for more information

Helen Sanderson Associates (2010) *Examples of Person Centred Medication Profiles.* www.helensandersonassociates.co.uk

Medicines and Healthcare Products Regulatory Agency (MHRA) (2008) *Medicines and Medical Devices Regulations: What you Need to Know.* www.mhra.gov.uk

Royal Pharmaceutical Society of Great Britain (2007) *The Handling of Medicines in Social Care.* www.rpharms.com

Royal College of Nursing (2009) *Dignity in Health Care for People with Learning Disabilities.* www.rcn.org.uk

Social Care Association (SCA) (2008) *Medication Administration in Social Care* www.socialcareassociation.co.uk

Chapter 5

Reducing the spread of infection

Sami's sister tells of an outbreak of diarrhoea and vomiting which recently occurred in the residential home where he lives. 'The home is always lovely and clean', she says, 'and they always wear aprons and things when they're serving food or are doing medicines, so it was a bit of a shock, but I suppose this sort of thing can happen anywhere. I think it was somebody who brought it in from outside.'

Introduction

Infection is spread by microscopic organisms such as viruses, bacteria, parasites and fungi that we can't see, unfortunately. So the first we know about them is when we get ill. Most micro organisms are harmless and our bodies have learned to fight others that are not. But some are more dangerous, or we're not accustomed to them, and they can lead to infections.

This chapter outlines procedures for reducing the spread of infection and your responsibilities for doing so.

Learning outcomes

This chapter will help you to:

- recognise the main routes by which infection gets into the body;
- understand your own role in reducing the spread of infection and supporting others to follow good practice;
- learn about effective hand hygiene;

▶

- learn about protective clothing, equipment and procedures and how and when to use them;

- be aware of the principles of safe handling of infected or soiled linen and clinical waste;

- understand how your own health or hygiene might pose a risk to others and ensuring that they don't;

- understand the importance of food safety, nutrition and hygiene;

- recognise the signs and symptoms of poor nutrition and hydration and how to promote good nutrition and hygiene.

This chapter covers:

Common Induction Standards – Standard 8 – Health and safety in an adult social care setting: Learning Outcome 7 and Learning Outcome 11

Level 2 HSC 027 – Contribute to health and safety in health and social care: Learning Outcome 4

Level 3 HSC 037 – Promote and implement health and safety in health and social care: Learning Outcome 4

The main routes by which infection gets into the body

The main routes by which infection enters the body are:

- through cuts or breaks in the skin – the skin acts as a barrier to infection, but cuts and broken skin allow infection to enter the body;

- down the digestive tract into the stomach or bowels, through swallowing food, drink or other infected products, usually resulting in vomiting and diarrhoea;

- down the respiratory tract into the lungs, e.g. colds, coughs, flu and other airborne infections are spread in this way;

- through body fluids (e.g. saliva, blood, semen), which are transmitted by injection or sexual contact and can remain localised (at the site of the infection) or enter the bloodstream.

Your employer's responsibilities for the control of infection

In organisations, employers must have in place 'systems to manage and monitor the prevention and control of infection. These systems use risk assessments and consider how susceptible service users are and any risks that their environment and other users may pose to them' (The Health and Social Care Act 2008: *Code of Practice for Health and Adult Social Care on the Prevention and Control of Infections and Related Guidance*).

The extent to which we succumb to or resist infection depends on many things, including:

- age – young children and older people are more susceptible;

- previous exposure to the infection or illness;

- chronic illness, which can reduce the efficiency of the immune system, something which is particularly relevant to some people with a learning disability;

- genetic abnormalities;

- medicines which suppress the immune system, such as steroids;

- surgery, because cuts and wounds enable the micro-organisms to enter the body;

- malnourishment, which can affect the immune system.

Several of the things listed above can put some people with a learning disability at greater risk of infection, especially those with complex health conditions.

In addition to undertaking risk assessment and putting control measures in place, employers must ensure:

- that the procedures are followed;

- that employees are trained in infection control;

- that the required recording and reporting measures are followed.

The control of infection is also governed by the Personal Protective Equipment Regulations 1992. The use of personal protective equipment is covered later in this chapter.

Your role in reducing the spread of infection

The spread of infection from one person to another is known as 'cross infection'. In a communal setting, such as a care home, nursing home, or day centre, steps can be taken to prevent cross infection. In public settings cross infection is more difficult to control, but following procedures to control infection will still help, for example washing your hands thoroughly. When working in someone's own home, you can help both yourself and the person you support to cut down on the risks of infection by being well informed and demonstrating good hygiene.

As a support worker you have a responsibility to avoid and reduce the spread of infection. Not only will this safeguard your own health, but also that of everyone around you, and it will additionally demonstrate good hygiene practices to your colleagues and the people you support.

Thinking point

How many times have you seen people either failing to wash their hands when they have used a public toilet, failing to dry their hands or rubbing their hands dry on their clothes and then going back into a public place?

In the light of what you have read above, what dangers do you think this poses in terms of cross infection?

Infection can be spread through body contact, (including hair) as well as through handling or touching equipment, clothing, linen and waste.

To fulfil your responsibilities as a support worker, there are several important things you can do to reduce the spread of infection:

- Be aware of your own role in supporting others to follow practices that reduce the spread of infection.

- Ensure you follow effective hand hygiene.

- Know how to use personal protective clothing, equipment and procedures and apply this knowledge appropriately and consistently.

- Understand how your own health and hygiene might pose a risk to others and how to avoid this.

Your own role in supporting others to prevent the spread of infection

These are the key points of your role:

- Follow the correct hygiene and other infection control practices as specified by, or agreed with, your employer, for example: getting first aid help for cuts; following good food preparation and management rules; not coming to work when you have an infectious illness, etc.

- Explain infection control policy and procedures in ways which are accessible to the people you support, for example by breaking your explanation down into manageable steps and explaining in appropriate language; by communicating in accessible ways – easy read, pictures or demonstration.

- Make sure you are familiar with, and follow, policy and procedures in relation to infection control.

- Help the person you support to learn correct hygiene practices and ways of preventing cross contamination, for example: rules for working in the kitchen, preparing food; how to act when you have a cold; and when it is better to stay at home and away from other people if you have an infectious illness.

- Encourage your colleagues and the people you support through your own good practice.

Activity

If you work in an organisation:

List activities or situations in your day to day work that are most likely to spread infection, for example through person to person contact, handling infected material, etc. Discuss some of these activities or situations with two of your colleagues, in particular:

- *How could these activities spread infection?*
- *How can your employer's control measures stop infection spreading in these activities or situations?*

Did you all mention the same things or were there differences in your understanding?

If you work in someone's home:

Discuss your chosen activities with one or two of the other support workers in your team or with other colleagues who are undertaking health and safety training or with your supervisor.

Effective hand hygiene, protective clothing, equipment and procedures

Hands are a major route for the spread of infection. Tests on people's hands in hospitals and family homes have found large numbers of bacteria. If we don't wash our hands regularly and thoroughly we can pick up and pass on infections through ordinary everyday activities. Depending on the type of support work you do and the setting in which you work, there may be even more chance of spreading infection through activities like personal care, managing health needs, preparing food and dealing with waste. Hand washing, done properly, is a highly effective measure for reducing the spread of infection.

How to wash your hands thoroughly

Here are five steps to thorough hand washing:

1. Wet hands under warm running water. (You can re-infect your hands if you use water stored in a basin.)
2. Apply a hand washing agent such as liquid soap from a dispenser or hand soap and create a lather.
3. Rub your hands together vigorously for 10 to 15 seconds, palms and backs of the hands, along and between fingers and thumbs.
4. Rinse soap off thoroughly under the running water.
5. Dry your hands thoroughly with a paper towel or warm air dryer, trying to avoid a cloth towel which others have used as this might be contaminated.

Always wash your hands thoroughly in the following situations:

- after using the toilet;
- after coughing, sneezing or blowing your nose;
- before and after preparing food;
- before and after eating;
- after feeding a pet or cleaning up after it;
- before starting and after finishing your support work.

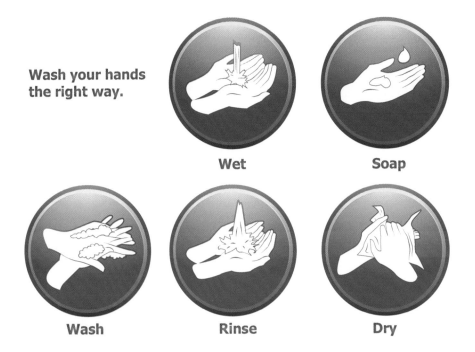

Wash your hands the right way.

Wet

Soap

Wash

Rinse

Dry

Always wash your hands thoroughly.

Protective clothing, equipment and procedures

Protective clothing provides an effective barrier to infection. You should wear disposable gloves and a disposable apron when:

Always wear protective gloves as an effective barrier to infection.

- you have to assist someone with toileting and deal with body fluids such as urine, faecal matter, vomit, blood, sweat, mucus or any other body fluids;

- you handle and dispose of soiled dressings, pads or linen;

- you have contact with anyone who has a rash, an open cut or broken skin, pressure sore, or who is menstruating.

You should wash your hands before and after carrying out any of these tasks to ensure further protection. Contaminated waste materials such as dressings, pads, needles and soiled linen should be disposed of in the bins provided for this purpose.

Supporting others to reduce the spread of infection

You also have a responsibility to help the person you support to follow procedures that reduce the spread of infection. Your role is to do this by:

- demonstrating good hygiene practices yourself at all times;

- supporting them in following good practice, such as correct hand washing; safe disposal of waste; thorough cleaning of surfaces especially in bathrooms and kitchens;

- making this information available to people in ways they can understand and follow.

Pictures and symbols can encourage people to follow good personal hygiene routines.

For example, you might need to provide more accessible instructions for when and how to wash hands, depending on the communication systems the person uses. For some, ordinary verbal explanations will be sufficient. With others you may have to use simpler language, pictures or symbols, such as Makaton. Some people will need encouragement and constant reminders. Others will need help to wash their hands or may need you to do it for them.

Situations that require special management

You may also have to deal with situations in which you have contact with someone who has an infectious illness or one that requires special management, for example a person with hepatitis, food poisoning or measles, or someone who is recovering from surgery. Your employer should have procedures to manage such situations and you should make sure you know them and follow them precisely. As well as wearing gloves and aprons, you may also have to wear other protective clothing, such as masks or gowns, and take other special precautions. Masks are only worn when there is a risk of airborne infections. They can be unsettling and even frightening for the people you support, so if you do need to wear one you will need to explain why to the person you support. Your employer should have guidelines to be followed if wearing masks is necessary at any time in your work setting.

Working in someone's own home

If you are working in someone's home and are employed by a care provider, you should be trained in infection control and provided with protective clothing such as gloves and aprons.

If you are employed directly by the person you support or his or her relative, infection control is just as important, for the person's sake, your own and that of any other people involved in his or her care or life. It should be part of the support plan and should be covered in your training. How this is done will depend on the person and his or her particular wishes or needs. Obviously you must be sensitive to the person's wishes, avoid intrusion and avoid making your support inappropriate and clinical. If your work involves intimate personal or health care, for example with someone who has profound and multiple disabilities or a particular health need and who uses a catheter or a stoma bag or is PEG fed, you will need specialised training and infection control will be an important part of this.

Equipment and infection control

Infection can also be spread through surfaces which have been contaminated, such as on a commode, walking frame, stand aid or hoist, so you need to follow your employer's procedures for reducing the spread of infection through equipment. This might include washing large pieces of equipment with antiseptic solution or sterilising some instruments.

Activity

Prepare a plan setting out how you would explain the importance of hand washing and other measures for infection control to someone you support. What kinds of resources would you use? Pictures, charts, leaflets, etc.?

Discuss your ideas with your line manager or at your next team meeting.

The safe handling of infected and clinical waste

In an organisation your employer must have procedures for handling and disposing of waste. The disposal system commonly used for this is colour coded as follows:

- Yellow for clinical waste;
- Red for soiled linen;
- Blue for recyclable instruments and equipment.

Where you support someone in their own home and the person is generally well, the domestic waste system should be used. Should there be any doubt about the disposal of waste, you should get advice from the local authority or from your employer. Some local authorities provide laundry services for people with bladder or bowel problems while others provide additional refuse collection.

Ensuring that your own health and hygiene do not pose a risk to others

Good personal hygiene can prevent you spreading infection, e.g. through your skin, hair and clothing, through leaving germs on surfaces, etc. Good personal hygiene includes:

- bathing or showering daily;
- using deodorant;
- washing your hair regularly;
- wearing clean clothes and shoes;
- tying long hair back;
- thorough hand washing as specified earlier in this chapter and on all necessary occasions.

The safe use of protective clothing and equipment, and adherence to the correct procedures for using them during personal care, when attending to someone who is ill and in the management of waste, will help protect your own health and that of others and prevent the spread of infection.

In addition you should follow these steps:

- Avoid wearing personal jewellery when carrying out personal care tasks in case you inadvertently injure someone or spread infection.
- Do not carry sharp objects in your pockets in case they cause injury to yourself or others.

- Stay at home if you have an infectious illness such as a cold, flu, sickness or diarrhoea.

- If you have a communicable illness stay away from work until your doctor clears you to return to work.

Thinking point

Do you have any concerns about infection control in your workplace? For example, are procedures not being followed correctly? Is the level of cleanliness in some places good enough? This isn't an easy thing to tackle, but it is important to talk to your manager or other relevant person if you have concerns about infection control.

Key points from this chapter

- The main routes by which infection gets into the body are through cuts in the skin, the digestive tract, the respiratory tract and through body fluids.

- As a support worker you have a responsibility to follow your employer's policies and procedures to reduce the spread of infection and in encouraging others, including the person you support, to follow good practice.

- Good hand hygiene, especially thorough hand washing after any activity which might involve infection, is an effective way of reducing the spread of infection.

- You can help reduce the spread of infection by making sure that:

  - you know how and when to wear or use protective clothing, equipment and procedures;

  - you are aware of the principles of safe handling of infected or soiled linen and clinical waste;

  - your own health or hygiene do not pose a risk to others.

References and where to go for more information

Department of Health (DH) (2010) *The Health and Social Care Act 2008: Code of Practice for Health and Adult Social Care on the Prevention and Control of Infections and Related Guidance.* www.dh.gov.uk

Health and Safety Executive (HSE) (2005) *A Short Guide to the Personal Protective Equipment at Work Regulations 1992.* www.hse.gov.uk

Pamis (2011) *Understanding and Managing Nutrition for People with Profound and Multiple Learning Disabilities.* www.pamis.org

Thurman, S (2011) *Communicating Effectively with People with a Learning Disability.* Exeter: BILD/Learning Matters

United Kingdom Home Care Association (UKHCA) (2009) *Effective Hand Washing for Homecare Workers, Version 3.* www.ukhca.co.uk

Chapter 6

Food safety, nutrition and hydration

The Corner Cafe is a cafe run by people with a learning disability with the support of staff from a local organisation. Health and safety is obviously extremely important and people are trained in all aspects of food safety and food hygiene. Inspections by the environmental health services of their local council have shown that they are achieving good standards of practice in all areas of their work and they have recently achieved the 'Eat Safe' award.

Introduction

As a support worker you are likely to be involved in some way with food – making or serving meals or snacks, disposing of leftovers, advising on or encouraging healthy eating. This chapter focuses on your role in promoting food safety, food hygiene, good nutrition and good hydration.

Understanding the importance of food safety and hygiene

It's almost impossible *not* to be aware of the risks of food poisoning from unsafe food, with outbreaks being publicised on television, in newspapers and on the internet. While sickness and diarrhoea can be debilitating for people whose health is generally good, it can be life threatening for older people or those with chronic health conditions.

Legislation

Food safety and hygiene legislation in the UK has had to be amended to meet the requirements of the European Union. The key legislation which applies to all nations of the UK is the Food Safety Act 1990, amended by the Food Safety Act (Amendment) Regulations 2004, which sets out the general principles and requirements of food law in EU states. The different nations of the UK all have additional food safety and food hygiene regulations which can be accessed at the website of the Food Standards Agency, at www.food.gov.uk

Maintaining food hygiene and food safety

As discussed in Chapter 5, infection spreads easily and quickly if we don't pay attention to hygiene. Cross contamination is one of the most common causes of food poisoning, transferring harmful bacteria from one food product to another through contaminated tools, equipment, surfaces or hands. Thorough cleaning is essential to get rid of harmful bacteria and to prevent bacteria from spreading.

The guidelines below apply to all organisations which handle food of any kind, including snacks, but many of them are also applicable to you if you work in someone's home, as you have the same responsibility for maintaining high standards of hygiene, reducing infection and preventing illness wherever you work. The difference is that whereas in an organisation food safety policy and procedures will be more formal and standards will be inspected by the regulating body, work in someone's home will be less formal and food safety will be part of agreed ways of working rather than formal policy.

Food hygiene

High standards of food hygiene are maintained by careful attention to the following areas:

- Paying attention to your own cleanliness and hygiene, as discussed in the previous chapter. We carry harmful bacteria on or in our skin, eyes, nose, throat, stomach and mouth; good personal hygiene can prevent us transferring these to foods and settings in which food is managed.

- Avoiding the preparation or handling of food if you have an infectious disease, such as diarrhoea, head cold, infected wounds, cuts, sores or other skin infections.

- Making sure you have been clear of symptoms for 48 hours before returning to work after a bout of diarrhoea or vomiting.

- Regular and thorough hand washing.

- Separating raw, cooked and ready to eat foods while shopping, preparing or storing food.

- Ensuring thorough cleanliness in the settings in which food is prepared, managed, served and stored, including work surfaces, floors, containers, utensils, pots and pans, knives, etc. Common places known to harbour large numbers of bacteria include fridge and freezer handles, taps, work surfaces, chopping boards, bin lids and tin openers.

- Wearing protective clothing, such as aprons, gloves or caps.

- Washing and drying cloths, tea towels and hand towels regularly and replacing them when worn or torn.

- Using paper towels and disposable cloths whenever possible.

- Using different utensils and equipment for different types of food – this means different boards and different knives for preparing vegetables and meat.

- Washing fruits, vegetables, salad ingredients and rice.

Cross contamination will occur when raw food touches or drips onto other food, equipment or surfaces, as well as when people handle it. Harmful bacteria also occur commonly in raw eggs, dust, dirt, soil and pets, so you need to take special precautions with these.

> ### Thinking point
>
> *Look back over the information above. Which things were you already aware of and which are new to you? How will this affect your food handling activities?*

Coloured chopping boards

Colour coded boards can help prevent the transfer of harmful bacteria by reminding you which boards are reserved for which type of food. The usual codes used in the UK are:

Red for raw meat
Yellow for cooked meat
Blue for raw fish
Green for salads and fruit
Brown for root vegetables
White for bakery and dairy products

In someone's home, even having two or three separate coloured boards to separate raw meat from other foods will help minimise the risk of food poisoning.

Food storage

Foods need to be stored at the right temperature, in the right place and in the right way to avoid cross contamination and bacteria multiplying. For example:

- Follow the storage instructions on packaged products, which tell you how they should be stored, whether they can be frozen and for how long, and what the 'use by' dates are.

- Refrigerate perishable foods promptly.

- Chill foods properly to stop bacteria multiplying.

- Do not put hot foods in the fridge.

- Check fridge temperatures regularly: food hygiene regulations recommend that fridges should be kept at between 2 and 5 degrees Centigrade and freezers at −18 degrees Centigrade or lower.

- Store raw meat at the bottom of the fridge to stop it dripping on anything.

- Do not store raw and cooked meats on the same shelf.

- All stored food should be labelled, dated and covered or kept in a closed container.

Michael supports Jack with meal planning, but it's Megan who helps him with his cooking. It was discovered that food was being thrown out nearly every day because it was past its sell-by date. An essential precaution, but a costly one. Better communication between workers and discussions with Jack about freezing foods and forward planning helped solve the problem – and cut down on costs.

Stuart was getting upset because he said support workers were throwing his food away. Supervision helped the workers to realise that they had to explain about sell-by dates sensitively and in ways Stuart could understand and not just say quickly in passing, 'You have to throw this out – it's past the sell-by date.'

Cooking and serving food

Here are some guidelines for maintaining food safety when you are cooking:

- Thaw frozen food in the fridge when you are ready to use it, apart from frozen packaged food where instructions say it can be cooked from frozen.

- Keep chilled food out of the fridge for as short a time as possible during preparation.

- Make sure food is thoroughly cooked so that all harmful bacteria are killed.

- Serve food immediately after it has been cooked.

- Make sure that food is hot all the way through.

- Check that meat juices are clear.

- Do not shorten cooking times.

- Avoid recipes which contain raw eggs which won't be cooked, such as mayonnaise and some puddings.

- Use a food thermometer rather than guessing the temperature of cooked food.

Disposing of food

Correct food disposal also prevents cross contamination and illness. This includes:

- clearing up all spillages immediately;

- disposing of leftover food immediately;

- emptying bins frequently;

- keeping food waste in containers that can be closed.

It is important to understand food safety and hygiene in the preparation of food.

The following rules apply in all organisations:

- There must be adequate facilities for storing and disposing of food waste and other rubbish, in an environmentally friendly way according to EU regulations.

- Equipment must be cleaned and disinfected where necessary to avoid cross contamination and kept in good repair.

- Equipment should be fitted where necessary with an appropriate control device, e.g. a temperature sensor.

Activity

Make a list of all the occasions when you deal with food in your work situation.

Choose one situation in which there have been, or could be, any difficulties in relation to food safety or hygiene. Describe the difficulties.

Describe what you can do to improve food safety or hygiene in this situation.

Describe how you would explain these safety measures to a person you support, including any resources you have used or would use.

Discuss your ideas with your line manager or a family carer, as relevant.

The importance of good nutrition and hydration in maintaining well being

We all know that food and water are fundamental to survival, so it's not surprising that helping people to eat and drink well is an important part of your job. For people with health problems of any kind, good nutrition and hydration are even more important.

Thinking point

Why might good nutrition and hydration be particularly important to people who have chronic or complex health problems?

Why good nutrition is important

Good nutrition means:

- having a balanced diet;
- eating enough for our level of activity, but not over-eating;
- eating the right foods.

A balanced diet is important because:

- it helps us to maintain a healthy weight;
- it provides us with everything the body needs for fitness and wellbeing, including:
  - carbohydrates for energy from foods like fruits, vegetables, breads, pasta, and dairy products;
  - calcium from dairy products to keep bones and teeth strong;
  - amino acids, from the proteins in meat, dairy products, eggs, fish, poultry, etc. which build and repair different parts of the body such as our immune system, muscles, hormones, nervous system and organs;
  - fats for the brain and hormones;
  - vitamins and minerals for energy, vision, metabolism and the immune system;
  - antioxidants from fruits and vegetables which help protect the body from damage from the sun, pollution and some illnesses.

Good nutrition also helps to prevent serious illnesses such as heart disease, stroke, diabetes, some cancers and some chronic illnesses.

The NHS advises us on how to achieve a balanced diet. You can find out more at www.nhs.uk/LiveWell

We should:

- base our meal on starchy foods as these give us energy – cereals, pasta, rice and bread (wholemeal if possible) and potatoes;

- eat plenty of fruit and vegetables – at least five a day;

- eat more fish – at least two portions a week, one of which should be oily fish such as salmon, mackerel, trout, herring, fresh tuna, sardines and pilchards;

- cut down on sugar and saturated fats, found in hard cheese, cakes, biscuits, sausages, cream, butter;

- eat less salt to reduce risks of high blood pressure, heart disease and stroke – no more than 6 grams a day for adults;

- drink plenty of water;

- always eat breakfast – it gives us the energy we need for the day.

The eatwell plate

Use the eatwell plate to help you get the balance right. It shows how much of what you eat should come from each food group.

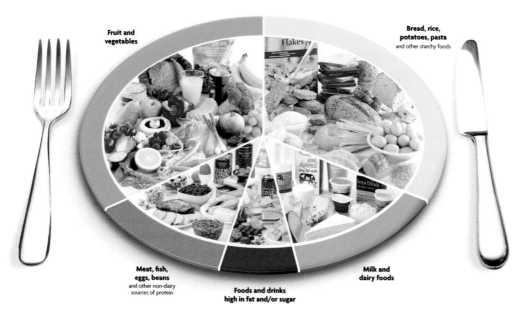

Department of Health in association with the Welsh Assembly Government, the Scottish Government and the Food Standards Agency in Northern Ireland

A balanced diet for vegetarians

The NHS also provides information on healthy eating for people who are vegetarians at www.nhs.uk/Livewell/Vegetarianhealth

Nutrition and people with a learning disability

There may also be particular reasons why some people with a learning disability have difficulties with nutrition, particularly those with complex health needs. A report by the Caroline Walker Trust (Crawley, 2007) focuses on nutritional health, food choice and healthy eating with specific reference to people with learning disabilities. The report identifies various factors which can contribute to poor nutritional health for people with a learning disability, amongst which are:

- physical and dental health problems and difficulties with eating, chewing or swallowing, which may affect food choice and the ability to eat well unaided;

- lack of experienced skilled staff, specialist eating and drinking equipment or insufficient support at mealtimes, especially for slow eaters or those who require modified texture foods;

- digestive problems such as gastro-oesophageal reflux disorder, and bowel problems such as constipation and diarrhoea which may deter people from eating because of the unpleasant consequences;

- sensory impairments and the need to rely on others when eating which may reduce enjoyment at mealtimes;

- medication which may have an effect on appetite;

- lack of understanding and accessible information about the need for a balanced diet;

- communication difficulties which may affect the person's ability to express food and eating preferences or professionals' ability to understand or express things in an accessible way;

- poverty and social exclusion.

People with complex health and/or particular dietary needs

You may be working with someone whose dietary requirements and/or methods of feeding are more specialised. This could be a person who has difficulty swallowing and who requires blended food or particular help with eating; someone with diabetes; or a person who requires PEG feeding. If this is the case, you will need special training from a professional and, where relevant, the person's family carer.

Religion, culture and food

You may also be supporting someone whose religious or cultural background has a bearing on what, when and how they eat. If you are, you need to make sure you are properly informed, through consultation with your employer, the person concerned and, where relevant, the person's family carer. You must also ensure that you follow your organisation's policy and procedures, or the agreed ways of working if you are employed by the person you support. Dietary or cultural requirements may also include which foods the person can and cannot eat, how food must be prepared, periods of fasting the person wishes to adhere to, as well as rules about alcohol.

You must consider a person's religious and cultural background when supporting them with eating and drinking.

Why good hydration is important

Water makes up about 60 to 70% of our body weight and has several important functions:

- maintaining and regulating body temperature;

- carrying nutrients and moving waste products through the body;

- lubricating joints;

- enabling all parts of the body to function properly, including the brain.

Regular intake of water is essential for good health and can help to lower the risk of common conditions such as:

- constipation;

- urinary tract infections;

- gallstones;

- dry and itchy skin;

- dry coughs.

Some studies have linked adequate hydration to the prevention of stroke, asthma, and bladder and colon cancers.

The Food Standards Agency recommends that adults drink between 6 and 8 glasses of fluid a day (approximately $1\frac{1}{2}$ litres) to prevent dehydration, although it is recognised that factors like body weight, size and level of activity help determine individual requirements. In hotter temperatures we need to drink more.

Activity

Prepare a plan to help someone you support understand more about healthy eating. Use a variety of accessible resources, such as photographs, leaflets, DVDs, etc. Discuss your plan with your manager or a family carer, as relevant, and, if it is appropriate, try it out and see how well it works. Do you need to change it in any way? Could you use it with other people?

Recognising the signs and symptoms of poor nutrition and hydration

Signs of poor nutrition

Whereas good nutrition promotes good physical and mental health, poor nutrition contributes to illness and even death. The symptoms of poor nutrition range from minor to severe and include:

- dry skin and hair and brittle nails;
- bad breath;
- constipation and digestive problems;
- blurred vision, inflamed eyes and eye infections;
- anaemia;
- fatigue;
- irritability and depression;
- insomnia;
- low blood pressure;
- problems with the immune system.

Signs of dehydration

When our water intake is less than we require we become dehydrated. The effects of even mild dehydration can be significant in young children, older people and people whose general health is poor. If you have ever seen the change in someone rehydrated intravenously (through a drip) in hospital, after a period of dehydration, you will be well aware of the power of water. People who have continence problems will often cut down the amount of liquid they drink, which leaves them at even greater risk of dehydration.

Dehydration can be mild, moderate or severe. The symptoms of mild to moderate dehydration include:

- thirst;
- dizziness or light headedness;
- dry lips, mouth and eyes;
- headache;
- tiredness;
- darker (concentrated) urine;
- passing only small amounts of urine infrequently (less than three or four times a day);
- lack of energy.

Moderate dehydration can be reversed without medical attention by drinking more fluids. However, if dehydration continues, it can:

- affect kidney function, e.g. cause kidney stones;
- cause liver, joint and muscle damage;
- cause cholesterol problems;
- cause constipation.

Severe dehydration signals a medical emergency so you should summon medical assistance urgently if the person you support shows any of the following symptoms:

- a weak pulse;
- a rapid heartbeat;
- an inability to urinate or long periods without passing urine;
- sunken eyes;
- seizure;
- a low level of consciousness;
- confusion;
- blood in stools or vomit.

Severe dehydration can be fatal if left untreated. The person requires admission to hospital and rehydration through a drip.

> **Thinking point**
>
> *Most of us know we should drink more water and other liquids that keep us hydrated but it's easy to forget in a busy life. Have you ever felt in yourself, or seen in someone else, the effects of dehydration?*
>
> *Try thinking about and improving your own hydration over the next week and see how you feel. Have you discussed hydration with a person you support? If not, how could you do this?*

How to promote good nutrition and hydration

Very poor levels of nutrition and severe dehydration can be life threatening, so it is essential for you to be well informed so that you can make sure the person you support learns as much as possible about good nutrition and hydration. Here are some ways in which you can encourage good nutrition and hydration:

- being a good role model by knowing about good nutrition and eating healthily;

- providing information about a balanced diet and doing this in ways which suit the needs of the person you support – you can do this by using all opportunities for discussion about healthy eating, such as going out to eat, watching food programmes on television;

- if you're involved in cooking, making sure the focus is on healthy foods;

- encouraging and supporting activity and appropriate exercise;

- explaining the importance of drinking enough water and other liquids that support good hydration;

- making good use of the social aspect of eating and planning meals – doing this with other people can help people to make healthy choices;

- encouraging pride in appearance and reinforcing this;

- involving family and friends, where appropriate, to provide extra support;

- encouraging and supporting interest and participation in cookery classes, health and fitness activities, etc.;

- growing vegetables and other foods;

- making meals more interesting – healthy eating shouldn't mean boring or limited choices.

Key points from this chapter

- Food safety is governed strictly by the Food Safety Act 1990 and the Food Safety Act (Amendment) Regulations 2004, which set out the general principles and requirements of food law in EU states.

- High standards of food hygiene, storage and disposal in the work setting promote good health, prevent cross contamination, serious illness and possibly even outbreaks of food poisoning.

- Good nutrition and hydration are essential for general wellbeing and overall health and can be achieved through a balanced diet, exercise and drinking enough water to keep the body well hydrated.

- It is important to recognise the signs of poor nutrition and hydration in order to take action to enable people to improve their level of wellbeing and, in some situations, prevent serious and life threatening illnesses.

References and where to go for more information

BBC Health (2012) *Nutrition* www.bbc.co.uk/health

Crawley, H (2007) *Eating Well: Children and Adults with Learning Disabilities.* www.cwt.org.uk

DiMascio, F, Hamilton, K and Smith, L (2011) *The Nutritional Care of Adults with a Learning Disability in Care Settings.* Birmingham: British Dietetic Association. www.bda.uk.com

Food Standards Agency (2007) *Eat Well. Your Guide to Healthy Eating.* www.food.gov.uk

Food Standards Agency (2009) *Food Safety Act 1990: A Guide for Food Businesses.* www.food.gov.uk

Food Standards Agency (2012) *Food Law Code of Practice.* www.food.gov.uk

NHS Choices (2010) *Eight Tips for Healthy Eating.* www.nhs.uk/LiveWell

NHS Choices (2011) *Healthy Eating for Vegetarians and Vegans.* www.nhs.uk/Livewell

NHS Choices (2011) *Dehydration.* www.nhs.uk

NHS Choices (2012) *A Balanced Diet.* www.nhs.uk/Livewell

NHS Scotland (2004) *Health Needs Assessment Report: People with Learning Disabilities in Scotland.* Glasgow: NHS Scotland

Pawlyn, J and Carnaby, S (eds) (2009) *Profound Intellectual and Multiple Disabilities: Nursing Complex Needs.* Chichester: Wiley Blackwell

Chapter 7

Safe moving and positioning

Christine has cerebral palsy and can transfer, but has difficulty with balance. She will sometimes fall when she is transferring, so needs to have someone by her side. She needs help getting into the shower, getting dressed, having compression bandages applied and compression stockings put on to control lymphoedema. She has an electric profiling bed to help her and her support workers help her with moving and positioning to avoid any injury. She uses her ILF (Independent Living Fund) budget to employ two support workers to help her mainly with moving and positioning and personal care.

Introduction

Helping people to move, or positioning them, while preserving their dignity requires skill, knowledge of and experience with the equipment they use, and a person centred approach to their care. Moving and positioning people is one of the most common causes of injury in the health and social care sector. So it's not surprising that this is an area that always requires specialist training. You need to be properly trained to avoid harm to yourself, the person you support and others.

The term used most in this book is 'moving and positioning', because this applies more appropriately to people, but 'moving and handling' is commonly used in documents and in legislation, so this term is used when referring to equipment.

Key legislation relating to moving and positioning

The Manual Handling Operations Regulations (1992) require employers to:

- *avoid* manual handling tasks where there is risk of injury 'as far as it is reasonably practical';

- *assess* the risks in tasks where moving and handling cannot be avoided;

- *reduce* the risks by putting appropriate measures in place.

As an employee you must:

- cooperate with your employer and follow systems of work laid down for your safety;

- make proper use of equipment provided to minimise the risk of injury;

- inform your employer of any hazards you identify;

- take reasonable care that, when involved in moving and positioning people or using equipment, your actions do not put you or others at risk.

The Health and Safety Executive identify two types of risk assessment required in health and social care settings: a *generic assessment* and an *individual assessment*.

The generic assessment should consider:

- the type and frequency of moving and positioning or handling tasks;

- overall equipment needs;

- staffing;

- the environment;

- the moving and positioning or handling that would be required in emergencies, e.g. fire evacuations or when someone falls.

The individual assessment should take account of the specific moving and positioning needs of the individual concerned, the type of support required and the risk to the person and support workers. This might involve the following kind of support: to transfer from bed to chair or wheelchair; to take a bath or shower; to use a stand aid or hoist; assistance with medical treatment, for example having to hold one position for a long time.

An individual risk assessment should be person centred, which means involving the person (and the family, where relevant) and should be done in a way that meets the person's needs and wishes. It should take into account:

- what the person is able and unable to do independently;

- the extent of the person's ability to support their own weight and any other relevant factors, for example pain, disability, spasm, fatigue, tissue viability or tendency to fall;

- the extent to which he or she can participate in or co-operate with transfers;

- whether he or she needs assistance to reposition and/or sit up when in their bed or chair and how this will be achieved, for example by using an electric profiling bed;

- the specific equipment needed and, if applicable, type of bed, bath and chair, as well as specific handling equipment, type of hoist and sling, sling size and attachments;

- the assistance needed for different types of transfer, including the number of staff needed – although hoists can be operated by one person, hoisting tasks often require two staff to ensure safe transfer;

- the arrangements for reducing the risk and for dealing with falls, if the person is at risk of these.

For more information go to the Health and Safety Executive website, at www.hse.gov.uk

Caroline, who's blind, explains how she trained her support workers to help her in her own house:

I told them I like to do things for myself but I need help with some things like pouring boiling water. I asked them not to move furniture around so that I'll know where it is and won't fall over it. I told them what it's like to be blind and how I can be safe in the house. I like to be guided by using their arm. But I don't want them to do everything for me – some staff want to do everything. I told them that I want to do things for myself – do my dishes, be independent. I can go to bed whenever I want – I don't need help getting into bed at night.

Charmaine, one of Caroline's support workers, highlights how important it is for all Caroline's workers to listen to what she wants and how she wants things done:

That's the way it has to be – it's Caroline's house – so that everything is the way Caroline wants it to be. We can't go about the house moving things.

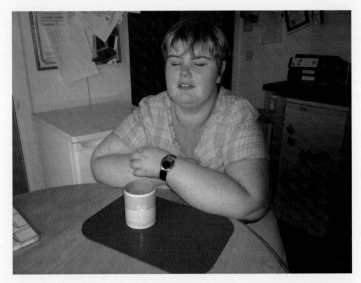

Individual assessments should take account of the specific moving and positioning needs of the person concerned.

Thinking point

Which kinds of moving and handling or positioning tasks do you undertake in your support work? What are the risks to you, the person or other people? What control measures have been put in place as a result of risk assessments?

Risk assessments should only be carried out by people who are suitably trained and assessed as competent. The assessment should balance the safety of employees and the safety and rights of the person being supported but should not curtail the individual's rights to autonomy, dignity or privacy.

The Health and Safety Executive recognises that 'there is no such thing as a completely safe manual handling operation. But working within the guidelines will minimise the risk and reduce the need for a more detailed assessment.' The diagram below identifies some of the factors which can affect risk.

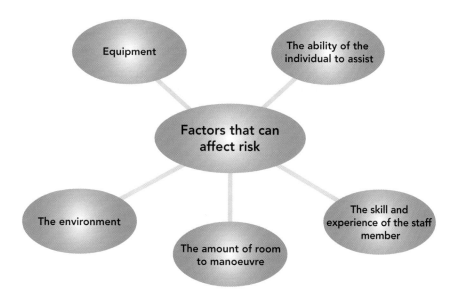

Risk assessment should also take account of the level of risk involved in moving and positioning, including:

- *low risk:* the person may be weight bearing and walking but requires assistance;

- *medium risk:* the person may be weight bearing for short periods, but can no longer walk and may require equipment;

- *high risk:* the person cannot weight bear and will require a considerable amount of assistance as well as equipment.

Working in someone's home

Many of the points discussed so far in this chapter will also apply if your work setting is someone's own home. You would not of course expect to have formal policies and procedures if you are employed by the person you support or a family carer, but you would have agreed on ways of working. You would also require manual handling training if your support work involved moving and positioning. This should be provided by a manual handling specialist.

Postural Care

The Postural Care Action Group has launched a campaign to raise awareness of the importance of good postural care for the thousands of people with multiple disabilities.

People who find it hard to move are most at risk of developing body shape distortions ... because they often sit and lie in limited positions. Postural care is about using the right equipment and positioning techniques to help protect and restore body shape. The earlier the intervention, the better – but it is never too late to start protecting someone's body shape.

Failure to protect body shape can have serious consequences for a person's health and quality of life. It can even cause premature death.

From www.pamis.org.uk

In addition to the Manual Handling Operations Regulations (1992), you also need to be aware of:

- the Provision and Use of Work Equipment Regulations 1998 (PUWER), which require employers to ensure that all equipment used in the workplace is suitable for the intended use, well maintained and in a safe condition, inspected regularly, used only by people suitably trained and competent and used in conjunction with relevant safety measures, e.g. safety warnings, protective devices;

- Lifting Operations and Lifting Equipment Regulations 1992 (LOLER), which came into effect in 1998, require that employers ensure that all equipment is sufficiently strong for the task, safe and fit for purpose, used safely in a well planned way, correctly positioned and installed, checked regularly and inspected where appropriate, that lifting tasks are planned, carried out by and supervised by competent people; equipment used for lifting and moving people must be inspected by a suitably competent person at least every six months or in accordance with a written scheme of examination;

- the Workplace (Health, Safety and Welfare) Regulations 1992 (WHSWR) which require that employers provide suitable working conditions for their employees.

The principles of safe moving and positioning

Here is a summary of what you should bear in mind when undertaking moving and positioning or handling tasks:

- Always follow health and safety policy and procedures, or agreed ways of working, in order to avoid injury to yourself, the person you are supporting and other people.

- Ensure that safe moving and positioning are appropriately covered in the person's support plan.

- Ensure that a risk assessment is in place and follow the procedures specified.

- Plan the task adequately, especially if you are inexperienced.

- Do not undertake tasks for which you have not had training.

- Always use the correct equipment and use it as instructed.

- Work with and involve the person you are supporting.

- Report any difficulties to your employer or line manager.

- Be aware of your own right to safety but balance this with the person's right to be moved safely, with dignity and with reassurance where required.

- Adopt a person centred approach to moving and positioning; this is discussed more fully below.

The Health and Safety Executive (HSE) offers general guidance on safe handling and positioning, as well as information on weights that can be safely lifted. Use the following activity to help you access this information.

Maintaining the person's dignity during moving and positioning

Preserving someone's dignity is an essential element of moving and positioning, especially as many tasks involve intimate personal care, so a person centred approach is essential. This means working in partnership with the person in the planning and execution of the task, including:

- building the task around the person's wishes and preferred ways of working, while taking care to work within health and safety requirements;

- ensuring that you wear suitable clothing and footwear for the task so that you do not put yourself or the person at risk;

- preserving high standards in your own personal hygiene, including washing your hands regularly, and not wearing jewellery;

- communicating appropriately with the person throughout the task – this means explaining what you are doing, checking that he or she is happy with how things are being done, but being sensible in how you do this so that you avoid inappropriate chatter;

- being sensitive to the person's feelings and ways of preserving dignity during more intimate tasks, including those that require undressing, toileting, being bathed or showered;

- being aware of religious and cultural requirements or constraints;

- taking account of gender and age, as well as individual differences in values and tolerances – what is acceptable to one person may not be appropriate for another;

- being sensitive to someone's fears and the effects on their dignity when they have to use certain types of equipment, such as hoists and stand aids to be put on the toilet or have help with cleaning themselves;

- stopping immediately if the person wants to stop or is becoming upset or distressed;

- seeking consent for any move and respecting the person's wishes if at all possible;

- encouraging the person to help themselves as far as possible rather than taking over yourself just because it's quicker or easier that way;

- helping the person do some of the more intimate tasks on their own, e.g. using a bed pan or having a bath.

Your own knowledge of and relationship with the person or people you support is a good guide to how you can promote and preserve their dignity. They themselves, as well as their family members where appropriate, are the best source of advice and support.

Activity

Describe some of the moving and positioning tasks you undertake with someone you support.

Explain how you use the person's risk assessment to keep yourself and the person safe.

Describe how you make sure your support is person centred – look back at the list above for help with this.

Moving and positioning tasks you are not allowed to carry out at your current stage of training

Moving and positioning people or moving and handling equipment requires specialist training for a number of reasons: to keep yourself and other people safe; to comply with legislation; and to enable you to use equipment competently and safely.

Training is generally referred to as 'manual handling' training and includes legal requirements and theory, as well as practical activities. You must be trained by a qualified moving and handling specialist, observed and signed off as competent. It is your responsibility to put your training into practice and comply with risk assessments relating to the task you are undertaking.

Until you receive and successfully achieve such training, you are not allowed to:

- use moving and positioning equipment such as stand aids, hoists, slide sheets, transfer boards, tracking systems;

- undertake any task you have not been trained for.

Moving and handling training should continue throughout your employment to make sure your skills and knowledge are up to date, in order to allow you to use pieces of equipment that are new to you and/or when you are working with someone you have not worked with previously. Just as risk assessment has to be individual as well as general, so some training will be specific to the individual person you are supporting. Even if you have been trained to use a particular piece of equipment, such as a hoist, you may have to undertake further training when you work with someone else who has particular needs.

After basic training and suitable experience, you may also have the opportunity to train as a manual handling risk assessor and later as a manual handling mentor. Your employer will be able to provide you with more information about this advanced training if it is something you are particularly interested in.

Key points from this chapter

- The Manual Handling Operations Regulations (1992) require employers to avoid, as far as is reasonably practical, manual handling tasks where there is a risk of injury; to assess the risks in tasks where moving and handling cannot be avoided; and to reduce the risks by putting appropriate control measures in place.

- The principles of safe moving and positioning include:
  - following the policies and procedures or agreed ways of working of your work setting in order to maintain safety and comply with legislation;
  - complying with risk assessment and control measures;
  - planning carefully;
  - undertaking only tasks for which you are trained;
  - reporting any difficulties;
  - adopting a person centred approach.

References and where to go for more information

References

Health and Safety Executive (HSE) (2011) *Getting to Grips with Manual Handling. A Short Guide.* www.hse.gov.uk

Health and Safety Executive (HSE) (2012) *Moving and Handling in Health and Social Care.* www.hse.gov.uk

Pamis (2012) *Postural Care Booklet & CD,* newsletter, February. www.pamis.org.uk

The PHACS Approach (2012) *Person Centred Handling and Assessment in Challenging Situations.* www.phacsapproach.com

The PHACS Approach (2012) *Moving and Handling Equipment Guide for the Disabled Person, Carers, and Advocates.* www.phacsapproach.com

Websites

Postural Care www.posturalcareskills.com

Chapter 8

Handling hazardous substances and materials

Maria works for a short breaks service and regularly has to support people who have profound and multiple learning disabilities, all of whom are wheelchair users.

David has come into the centre for two weeks. He needs considerable assistance with intimate personal care, including toileting, changing continence pads and bathing.

Maria has to be careful to follow all the policies and procedures the service has for handling and disposing of hazardous materials. This includes toilet and bath cleaners, floor cleaners, mops, and washing cloths as well as used continence pads.

Introduction

In the course of her work with David and other people who need support with personal care, Maria will almost certainly have to use substances and materials like the ones mentioned above, which have the potential to cause harm, which means they are *hazardous*. But she'll probably also come into contact with body fluids, soiled linen, pads and dressings. She has a responsibility to David and other people who use the service, to herself and to her co-workers to deal with hazardous substances and materials carefully and make sure that they do not cause any harm.

This chapter discusses the type of hazardous substances you might come into contact with in your work setting and provides information on their safe use, storage and disposal.

Hazardous substances in your work setting

Hazardous substances include products which contain chemicals, or give off vapours, fumes, mists or gases, as well as those which harbour germs. In your work setting, these might include such things as disinfectants, cleaning materials, garden pesticides, pet cleaning products, gas, body fluids, or pads and dressings containing body fluids (blood, urine, faeces, infected matter), and medication.

Thinking point

Which hazardous materials and substances do you use or come into contact with in your work? Are you aware of:

- *their potential for harm?*
- *your employer's policies and procedures, or agreed ways of working, for using and disposing of them?*
- *who you can ask if you have any questions and concerns?*

Safe practices for the use, storage and disposal of hazardous substances or materials

The use, storage and disposal of hazardous substances are all governed by the Control of Substances Hazardous to Health Regulations 2002 and the Control of Substances Hazardous to Health (Amendment) Regulations 2003 (COSHH). This legislation covers the use of chemicals (such as bleach), carcinogens (which are cancer-forming agents) and biological agents. The law defines hazardous substances as those which are toxic, corrosive, harmful or irritant, as well as biological agents (which harbour germs) and dusts in substantial concentrations. You can find out more at www.healthyworkinglives.com

Your employer's responsibilities for storing, using and disposing of hazardous substances

Where possible, an employer should prevent exposure to hazardous substances. They should, for example, determine if a safer process or substance can be used (a milder cleaning agent instead of an irritant one; a vacuum rather than a brush; a solid form instead of liquid or powder to avoid splashes and spills).

Where it is not possible to prevent exposure, control measures must be put in place and monitored to make sure they are used. This involves:

- identifying hazardous substances used in the work setting;
- carrying out risk assessments for these hazards;
- providing control measures, keeping these in good order and ensuring they are used;
- providing information, instruction and training for employees;
- providing monitoring and health surveillance, where this is necessary;
- planning for emergencies;
- reporting any accidents.

The Health and Safety Executive (HSE) identifies three things to think about when undertaking risk assessment for hazardous substances:

- What do you do that involves hazardous substances?
- How can these cause harm?
- How can you reduce the risk of harm occurring?

For more information go to **www.hse.gov.uk**

Since 2005, employers have been required to follow eight principles of good practice in the control of hazardous substances:

1. Design and operate processes and activities to minimise emission, release and spread of substances hazardous to health.

2. Take into account all relevant routes of exposure – inhalation, skin absorption and ingestion – when developing control measures.

3. Control exposure by measures that are proportionate to the health risk.

4. Choose the most effective and reliable control options which minimise the escape and spread of substances hazardous to health.

5. Where adequate control of exposure cannot be achieved by other means, provide, in combination with other control measures, suitable personal protective equipment.

6. Check and review regularly all elements of control measures for their continuing effectiveness.

7. Inform and train all employees on the hazards and risks from the substances they work with and the use of control measures developed to minimise the risks.

8. Ensure that the introduction of control measures does not increase the overall risk to health and safety.

From www.hse.gov.uk

In an organisation your employer, by law, has to keep a COSHH file which:

- is easily accessible to all staff;
- provides information about:
  - all hazardous substances used in your work setting;
  - their effects;
  - where they are stored;
  - how they are labelled;
  - how they should be dealt with;
  - how to deal with any emergency involving each particular substance.

The storage of hazardous substances

Safe storage is required for all hazardous substances. The safety data sheet, provided for all hazardous substances, gives workers and emergency services procedures for storing, handling and working safely with a substance. Safe storage includes such procedures as:

- correct labelling and suitable containers;

- storing substances in a separate, secure area, for example in a locked cupboard or store;

- storing substances under the correct conditions as specified in the safety data sheet;

- in an organisation, keeping flammable materials in a fireproof store or cupboard if possible;

- limiting the amount of flammable material kept at any one time.

Labelling and information relating to hazardous substances

The European Regulation (EC) No 1272/2008 on classification, labelling and packaging (CLP) of substances and mixtures came into force in all EU member states, including the UK, on 20 January 2010. The CLP Regulation:

- adopts in the EU the Globally Harmonised System (GHS) on the classification and labelling of chemicals;

- is being phased in through a transitional period which runs until 1 June 2015. The CLP Regulation applies to substances from 1 December 2010, and to mixtures (preparations) from 1 June 2015;

- applies directly in all EU member states. This means that no national legislation is needed;

- is overseen by the European Chemicals Agency (ECHA);

- will replace the Chemicals (Hazard Information and Packaging for Supply) Regulations 2009 – CHIP – from 1 June 2015.

New symbols will be introduced which are similar to the CHIP hazard symbols – they have a new shape, new design and a new colour. Here are some examples.

The new CLP hazard symbols.

For more information go to www.hse.gov.uk

Manufacturers of hazardous products have to:

- describe the risk;
- state the level of risk associated with the product;
- describe how the product should be used;
- describe how the product should be stored safely.

By law, suppliers of chemicals must provide a safety data sheet providing information on handling, storing and emergency measures for the chemical. The safety data sheet provides guidance which helps with risk assessment for the substance involved.

Your responsibility when dealing with hazardous substances

As a support worker you have a duty of care to ensure that any hazardous substances you work with are stored, used and disposed of safely. Before you use, store or dispose of any substance you know to be hazardous, or suspect might be hazardous, you should:

- check the container for a hazard symbol, and if there is one:

  - either read your organisation's COSHH file and ensure you are familiar with procedures for dealing with the substance, e.g. wearing protective clothing, clearing up spillages immediately, putting up warning signs to keep others out of the area; or follow the manufacturer's instructions and agreed ways of working, if you work in someone's home;

  - report to your line manager or employer any questions or concerns about the particular substance or the way it is being used or stored.

The disposal of hazardous substances

Hazardous waste, as its name implies, can cause harm and/or spread infection, as discussed in Chapter 5, so you must make sure you are clear about its safe disposal.

For chemical waste, follow the instructions on the safety data sheet and your employer's procedures as set out in the COSHH file, if this is relevant to your work setting.

For other hazardous substances or materials, such as clinical waste, you must also follow the procedures set out for your work setting, or agreed ways of working. In an organisation this will involve the following materials and methods of disposal:

- Clinical waste such as used dressings: yellow bins or bags.
- Soiled linen: red bags.
- Recyclables such as instruments: blue bags.
- Body fluids: flush, then clean and disinfect area used.
- Needles, syringes and cannulas (used with drips and for giving medicines intravenously): yellow sharps box or bucket.

Working in someone's home

If you are employed by an agency to work in someone's home, your employing agency has responsibility for training you and providing information about their policies and procedures relating to the control of hazardous substances.

If your employer is the person you support, or a family carer, formal policies and procedures aren't always appropriate, but you will still need to agree ways of working when hazardous substances are concerned. For instance, if you provide support with continence pads or catheter bags you would need to have guidance on how to change and dispose of these in a way that doesn't cause any infection to yourself or the person. You also need to follow safe ways of using, storing and disposing of other potentially harmful materials, such as bleach, household cleaners and garden pesticides, for example. This would be similar to the procedures followed in any household, unless there were particular circumstances or substances involved. The important thing to remember is that you and the person who employs you still have responsibilities for the safe use, storage and disposal of any hazardous substances used in the work setting.

Activity

Over the next few days make a list of the hazardous substances you come into contact with in your work. Make brief notes on the safety procedures you apply in using, storing and disposing of these.

Discuss this list with your line manager or a senior colleague and ask for feedback, especially on how you can make any improvements. Discuss any issues or concerns you have.

Key points from this chapter

- Hazardous substances and materials are those that create risk to people's health; these are defined in law as substances which are toxic, corrosive, harmful or irritant, as well as biological agents (which harbour germs) and dust in substantial concentrations.

- The storage, use and disposal of hazardous substances are controlled by law, primarily by the Control of Substances Hazardous to Health Regulations 2002 and the Control of Substances Hazardous to Health (Amendment) Regulations 2003 (COSHH).

- You should ensure you are familiar with all the hazardous substances and materials you encounter in your work setting and the risk assessments and control measures associated with them.

- You must comply with your employer's policies and procedures, or agreed ways of working, for the storing, using and disposal of hazardous substances and materials, for example, by using protective clothing if required, storing in regulated conditions and disposing of substances in the specified containers and using the correct methods.

References and where to go for more information

European Commission. Enterprise and Industry (2008) *Chemicals. CLP legislation, guidance and archives.* http://ec.europa.eu

Health and Safety Executive (HSE) (2010) *Principles of Good Control Practice.* www.hse.gov.uk

Health and Safety Executive (HSE) (2011) *COSHH basics.* www.hse.gov.uk

Health and Safety Executive (HSE) (2012) *Control of Substances Hazardous to Health (COSHH).* www.hse.gov.uk

Health and Safety Executive (HSE) (2012) *What is a Substance Hazardous to Health?* www.hse.gov.uk

Healthy Working Lives (2012) *Hazardous Substances.* www.healthyworkinglives.com

Chapter 9

Fire safety in the work setting

When I was at college they had fire rescue areas – concrete areas – and I had to go there when the fire alarm went and wait there till the firefighters came. Somebody came with me. Everybody else could go down the stairs but I couldn't. I had an ID card so they always knew where I was. They had a kind of a blanket with handles (an evacuation sledge) that I had to lie in and they took me down the stairs in that. It was really scary.

Christine, who uses an electric wheelchair

Introduction

Fire drills save lives. Hundreds of people die in fires every year in the UK, so all employers need to take their responsibility for fire safety very seriously indeed, no less so when the people involved might not be able to move quickly, or might need help to move or follow instructions.

This chapter focuses on fire safety and fire prevention in services which support people with a learning disability, in organisations and in the person's own home.

Learning outcomes

This chapter will help you to:

- outline, understand and demonstrate measures that prevent fires from starting and spreading;

- explain emergency procedures to be followed in the event of a fire in the work setting;

- explain the importance of maintaining clear evacuation routes at all times and ensure that this happens.

This chapter covers:

Common Induction Standards – Standard 8 – Health and safety in an adult social care setting: Learning Outcome 8

Level 2 HSC 027 – Contribute to health and safety in health and social care: Learning Outcome 7

Level 3 HSC 037 – Promote and implement health and safety in health and social care: Learning Outcome 7

Fire safety and services for people with learning disabilities

There are many factors that need to be taken into consideration in services that provide support for people with learning disabilities. These include the nature of the service and the needs of the people being supported. For example:

- Is it a day or a residential service?
- How many of the people using the service have mobility impairments or additional health conditions?
- Is the service located in one building or in a number of different premises?
- Does support take place in people's homes or out in the community or both?

While fire safety regulations govern all services, the nature of the service, its location and the needs and number of the people concerned will have implications for fire safety.

This chapter provides general information on what you as a support worker need to know about fire safety regulations and procedures. However, each service has its own characteristics and requirements so you need to ensure that you are clear about how these apply in your own particular work setting, whether this is in an organisation or in someone's own home. Your best source of advice is your line manager if you work in an organisation, your local authority and local fire safety officers if you are employed by the person you support or a family carer. If you have any questions or concerns about fire safety or what to do in the event of a fire you should always seek expert advice.

The larger the service and the more complex the support needs of the people concerned, the more likely the need for specialist advice on fire safety.

> Premises with very large numbers of residents (e.g. greater than 60), or with complicated layouts (e.g. a network of escape routes, or split levels), or those of greater than four storeys, or which form part of a multi-occupied complex, will probably need to be assessed by a competent person who has comprehensive training or experience in fire risk assessment.
>
> *Fire Safety Risk Assessment: Residential Care Premises* www.communities.gov.uk

Measures that prevent fires from starting and spreading

You, your employer and the person you support all have responsibilities to do all you can to stop fires starting in the work setting and, if a fire does break out, to prevent it spreading. First, let's think about legal responsibilities and fire safety.

The law and fire safety

The Office of the Deputy Prime Minister is responsible for Fire Safety legislation in the UK. Key legislation includes:

- England and Wales: Regulatory Reform (Fire Safety) Order 2005
- Scotland: The Fire Scotland Act 2005; Fire Safety (Scotland) Regulations 2006
- Northern Ireland: Fire Safety Regulations (Northern Ireland) 2010

The emphasis in all these regulations is on risk assessment and management. This involves:

- identifying fire hazards and carrying out risk assessments;
- identifying the people, or groups of people at risk and anyone who may be especially at risk;
- removing and reducing the risks as far as reasonably possible;
- putting a plan in place for fire prevention and control;

- developing and implementing appropriate emergency procedures in the event of fire;

- keeping accurate records of fire hazards, risk assessment, actions taken etc.;

- reviewing risk assessments and procedures regularly and in the event of any changes to premises or work activity.

Local fire services should be involved in the development of the fire prevention and control plan as they are in the best position to advise on the needs in a particular work setting. The prevention and control plan should specify:

- what action someone should take on discovering a fire;

- how everyone on the premises will be warned in the event of fire;

- the procedures for evacuation;

- the location of fire-fighting equipment;

- the duties and identity of those persons who have specific roles;

- where everyone should assemble following evacuation;

- arrangements for summoning the fire and rescue service and meeting them on arrival.

The legislation does not apply in an individual's home, but the government has issued advice and guidelines for fire prevention and safety in the home. You can find out more about this by logging on to the fire safety section of www.direct.gov.uk

Guidance for care workers to help reduce monthly fire deaths

In 2012 the London Fire Brigade, together with Skills for Care, issued new guidance to organisations and individuals supporting people in their own home. Research by the London Fire Brigade identified that people living in their own home and in receipt of domiciliary or home care support are more at risk of injury or death because of a fire. The guidance recommends that support workers, their managers and the people they support, contact their local fire brigade for free advice on fire safety in the home.

The full report on *Fire Safety of People in Receipt of Domiciliary Care* can be read here: www.london.gov.uk

Fire and rescue services throughout the UK offer a range of fire safety services which can include:

- the provision and maintenance of smoke alarms;

- advice on making a fire action plan;

- safety advice on cooking;

- fire and fireworks safety advice.

You can get information about this from your local council.

Other pieces of legislation that are relevant are the Health and Safety at Work Act 1974 and the Equality Act 2010. Fire safety is also included in the requirements of the bodies which regulate health and social care in the different countries of the UK.

You will notice that fire safety legislation mentions people especially at risk, which includes people with a learning disability as well as any employees or others with particular needs – this could include wheelchair users, people with visual or hearing impairment and elderly people with impairments who might be on the premises. Risk assessments must be as thorough as possible and take full account of the range of needs of the people concerned. In services for people with a learning disability, needs can be considerable. For example, there may be several wheelchair users, people who are likely to become confused or frightened, or people who have challenging behaviours, or profound and multiple learning disabilities and are entirely dependent on others in terms of mobility. So fire safety has to be particularly rigorous. It is important that you acquaint yourself thoroughly with fire safety procedures in your own work setting, as discussed in more detail below.

Here are some recognised ways in which fires can be prevented or stopped from spreading. Some of these are your employer's responsibility, some are yours and some are shared by the employer, you and the person or people you support.

Your employer's responsibility for fire safety

In an organisation, your employer should:

- ensure that you are fully informed about any fire hazards, the fire safety risk assessment and the recommended measures to prevent fires and stop them spreading;

- install fire doors that are suitable for the setting and where appropriate, labels and notices, such as 'Fire door. Keep shut' to ensure that fire doors are not propped open;

- ensure that all rubbish is disposed of in the correct way and that piles of rubbish are not allowed to build up;

- ensure that highly flammable materials or substances, e.g. oxygen, are subject to special precautions, for example are kept in fire proof rooms or cupboards, and that you, any person using it and any others involved have been trained in its use;
- have regular fire drills, identify and report any problems and amend risk assessments and safety procedures as required;
- have a fire alarm which is properly designed, installed, properly managed and maintained to make sure it operates as it should.

Your responsibilities for fire safety

The type of setting you work in is particularly relevant to how legislation is applied, but there are some basic guidelines common to all work settings, as well as safe practices that can help prevent fires starting or spreading and enable you to respond in the correct way – and possibly prevent injury or death – if a fire does start.

If you work for an organisation, or agency, your employer must ensure that you are fully informed about the policies and procedures of the organisation and how these apply in your particular work setting. You must be clear about your own responsibilities to other people and to yourself, and cooperate fully with your employer's fire safety policies and procedures.

This means:

- being able to use fire safety equipment correctly;
- informing your employer of any dangers or issues that might not have been identified in risk assessment;
- knowing what action to take on discovering a fire;
- familiarising yourself with all escape routes;
- knowing the locations of fire extinguishers, their type and method of operation (see section below on fire fighting equipment).

If your support work is in someone's own home, and you are employed by a care provider, your employer should provide you with the relevant information, guidance and training. In situations where the person you support, or a family carer, is your employer, clear guidance on fire safety should be included in your induction and as part of the agreed ways of working.

Fire safety is also one of your responsibilities when supporting people in the community, if you are at the cinema, on holiday and staying in a hotel, having a day away at a tourist attraction and so on. You need to make sure you obtain information about fire exits, safety precautions and evacuation procedures and that you convey this information to the person you support and check that they have understood it. This is discussed further later in this chapter.

As a support worker you can promote fire safety by:

- undertaking training and putting it into practice where necessary;

- in someone's house, being aware of the fire hazards and undertaking, or contributing to, a fire safety risk assessment;

- in a house, encouraging the person to have smoke alarms which are checked regularly and enabling the person you support, where appropriate, to check them;

- providing fire prevention and safety information to the person you support in ways that are accessible and checking to see that these are understood, e.g. through discussion, having fire prevention speakers, using DVDs, preparing pictorial information etc. (This is particularly important in situations which are particularly prone to fires, such as in kitchens, when using electrical equipment, if there are overloaded electrical sockets, or when someone is a smoker. An easy read leaflet on fire safety in the home can be found at www.firekills.gov.uk and this may be helpful.);

- keeping exits free of obstacles;

- in someone's house, helping the person to make sure that any matches, lighters and other highly flammable materials are stored in a safe place; that candles and gas rings are not left unattended; that the person doesn't smoke in bed; that electric blankets are serviced and disposed of safely; that electrical appliances are checked and kept safe with no bare wires; that electric sockets are not overloaded, etc.

- in an organisation, reporting any additional hazards you identify.

Your training should contain information about all the fire hazards associated with the materials and equipment you use in your work, as well as any of your activities which might place you and others at risk of a fire (working in a kitchen for instance), the measures in place to prevent a fire and how to respond if a fire occurs. In an organisation you should also be made aware of who the designated people are who are responsible for different aspects of fire safety.

If a fire does start, you can stop it spreading by:

- making sure that doors and windows are closed;
- removing any combustible materials away from the fire if it is safe to do so.

But remember: safety should always be your first priority, for yourself and anyone else involved. Don't try to stop a fire spreading if there is any danger to yourself or other people – get yourself and others to a place of safety immediately, preferably out of the building if this is possible, or to a designated safe place as specified in the fire safety procedures for your work setting.

Activity

Think about your own work setting and the activities you are involved with. List the activities and the associated equipment which might present fire hazards, such as cooking, hair washing and drying etc.

Now list five ways you could take safety measures to prevent fire in these situations.

Explain how you would enable a person you support to understand the hazards and cooperate in preventing fire.

If you work for an organisation, check that what you say complies with your employer's procedures.

Fire fighting and fire safety equipment

Fire extinguishers

The use of a fire extinguisher can stop a small fire becoming a major one and can save lives. There are different fire extinguishers for different types of fire. All are red but each has a different coloured band according to the type of fire it is to be used for, and each has its purpose written on it. The different types of fire extinguishers and their use are shown below.

Fire blankets

Fire blankets are stored in a red container and are suitable for chip pan fires and clothing fires. A casualty can be rolled in the blanket to extinguish the fire and the blanket can also be used to extinguish a small fire, in a bin or chip pan, for example.

The extinguisher colour system

Extinguisher type and patch colour	Use for	Danger points	How to use	How it works
Red  Water	Wood, cloth, paper, plastics, coal, etc. Fires involving solids but **not** on chip or fat pan fires.	Do **not** use on burning fat or oil, or on electrical appliances.	Point the jet at the base of the flames and keep it moving across the area of the fire. Ensure that all areas of the fire are out.	Mainly by cooling burning material.
Blue Multi-purpose dry powder	Wood, cloth, paper, plastics, coal, etc. Fires involving solids. Liquids such as grease, fats, oil, paint, petrol, etc. but **not** on chip or fat pan fires.	Safe on live electrical equipment, although the fire may re-ignite because this type of extinguisher does not cool the fire very well. Do **not** use on chip or fat pan fires.	Point the jet or discharge horn at the base of the flames and, with a rapid sweeping motion, drive the fire towards the far edge until all the flames are out.	Knocks down flames and, on burning solids, melts to form a skin smothering the fire. Provides some cooling effect.

Extinguisher type and patch colour	Use for	Danger points	How to use	How it works
Blue Standard dry powder	Liquids such as grease, fats, oil, paint, petrol etc. but **not** on chip or fat pan fires.	Safe on live electrical equipment, although does not penetrate the spaces in equipment easily and the fire may re-ignite. This type of extinguisher does not cool the fire very well. Do **not** use on chip or fat pan fires.	Point the jet or discharge horn at the base of the flames and, with a rapid sweeping motion, drive the fire towards the far edge until all the flames are out.	Knocks down flames.
Cream AFFF (Aqueous film-forming foam) (multi-purpose)	Wood, cloth, paper, plastics, coal, etc. Fires involving solids. Liquids such as grease, fats, oil, paint, petrol, etc. but **not** on chip or fat pan fires.	Do **not** use on chip or fat pan fires.	For fires involving solids, point the jet at the base of the flames and keep it moving across the area of the fire. Ensure that all areas of the fire are out. For fires involving liquids, do not aim the jet straight into the liquid. Where the liquid on fire is in a container, point the jet at the inside edge of the container or on a nearby surface above the burning liquid. Allow the foam to build up and flow across the liquid.	Forms a fire-extinguishing film on the surface of a burning liquid. Has a cooling action with a wider extinguishing application than water on solid combustible materials.

Extinguisher type and patch colour	Use for	Danger points	How to use	How it works
Cream Foam	Limited number of liquid fires but **not** on chip or fat pan fires.	Do **not** use on chip or fat pan fires. Check manufacturer's instructions for suitability of use on other fires involving liquids.	Do not aim jet straight into the liquid. Where the liquid on fire is in a container point the jet at the inside edge of the container or on a nearby surface above the burning liquid. Allow the foam to build up and flow across the liquid.	Foams a fire-extinguishing film on the surface of a burning liquid.
Black Carbon dioxide CO_2	Liquids such as grease, fats, oil, paint, petrol, etc. but **not** on chip or fat pan fires.	Do **not** use on chip or fat pan fires. This type of extinguisher does not cool the fire very well. Fumes from CO_2 extinguishers can be harmful if used in confined spaces: ventilate the area as soon as the fire has been controlled.	Direct the discharge horn at the base of the flames and keep the jet moving across the area of the fire.	Vaporising liquid gas smothers the flames by displacing oxygen in the air.
Fire blanket	Fires involving both solids and liquids. Particularly good for small fires in clothing and for chip and fat pan fires, provided the blanket **completely** covers the fire.	If the blanket does not completely cover the fire, it will not be extinguished.	Place carefully over the fire. Keep your hands shielded from the fire. Take care not to waft the fire towards you.	Smothers the fire.

Systems and equipment in public buildings

Fire fighting equipment also includes systems used in public buildings for disabled people and anyone else who needs special assistance. Examples include sound enhancing systems such as loops, flashing beacons and vibrating pagers. In buildings with open public access, evacuation equipment is frequently available such as an evacuation chair.

You should take time to find out about the fire safety procedures in public buildings which are used by the person you support, especially about how the procedures are adapted to meet the needs of disabled people. If you are dissatisfied with what is in place, or feel staff are not well enough informed, you should discuss this with your line manager or other appropriate person. It may be possible for you and the person you support to help to improve fire safety in such buildings.

Evacuation chairs are often used for people needing special assistance.

Emergency procedures to be followed in the event of a fire in your work setting

If you work in an organisation, your employer must display information about what action to take in the event of a fire. This will be specifically designed for your work setting and should include such things as how to raise the alarm, inform others, get people to safety, access fire extinguishers, get to assembly points, get out of the building, etc. We can get so used to notices we see every day that we tend to ignore them, but you should make sure you are familiar with the information in your work setting.

Fire alarms are often used in work settings in the event of a fire.

If you work in an organisation, do you know where this information is displayed in your work place? Can you remember the instructions? If not, take some time to read them again and refresh your memory by reading them regularly. You have to act quickly if there is a fire so knowing what to do could save your own life and the lives of others.

If you work in someone's home, do you know what to do in the event of a fire? If not, make sure you find out as a matter of priority and that you discuss it with your employer.

You need to be very clear of your own role and responsibilities if a fire does occur. Your employer's fire safety procedures document is your best source of information about what to do in your own work setting. If you work in someone's home, this information should be in the agreed ways of working, or provided by your employer, whichever is relevant. Within a care home or other organised premises, your employer is responsible for keeping a register of who is present in the building in case of the need to evacuate. It is the responsibility of the organisation to maintain a register and employees need to comply with policies.

You need to know:

- how to raise the alarm if you discover a fire;
- how to respond if you hear the fire alarm;
- who will contact emergency services;
- where the fire assembly points are;
- how to help the people you support to move away from the danger area, including a person who is unable to move by themselves or anyone else who needs more specialised help.

It is likely that some people will become distressed if there is a fire, or if there is a possibility of one, especially if they have difficulty understanding what is going on or have challenging behaviours. If you support anyone you think might have particular difficulties in any emergency situation, it is good practice to discuss this with your line manager. Obviously it's not only people with a learning disability who might react badly to an emergency – any one of us could. It is good practice to think about and discuss the best ways of reassuring and supporting people should a fire or other emergency arise.

How much fire safety training, information or practice have you had in your own work setting? Write down the procedures you need to follow if a fire occurs.

Now look at a copy of the fire safety policy and procedures, or think about agreed ways of working, to see if you have left anything out.

Do you think there are any gaps in the guidance provided? Is there anything you are not clear about? If there is, make a point of discussing this with the relevant person, e.g. your line manager or the person who employs you.

Remember that prompt and correct action can save your own life and that of other people in the event of a fire, so don't put off clarifying anything you are not sure of.

Maintaining clear evacuation routes at all times

How quickly people can get out of a burning building can mean the difference between safety, severe injury or death, so plans for evacuating premises need to be clear, easy to follow and practised regularly. Evacuation routes that enable people to escape quickly and easily are vital.

Evacuation routes and procedures in health and social care settings

Regular fire drills are essential for giving people practice in knowing what to do and in uncovering any unidentified hazards. The people with particular responsibility for the different aspects of fire safety must monitor evacuation routes to ensure they are fit for the purpose of getting people out of the building quickly and efficiently. This is particularly important in health and social care settings, where there are likely to be many individuals who depend on the support of others to move around.

In an organisation, the employer has a responsibility to inform and train all employees in how to leave the building. This includes training in how to evacuate people with mobility impairment and the use of any evacuation equipment. You and your colleagues also have responsibility for knowing about the evacuation routes and evacuation procedures to follow. You have a responsibility to cooperate precisely with procedures, to ensure that the people you support are clear about evacuation procedures and to support them in carrying these out.

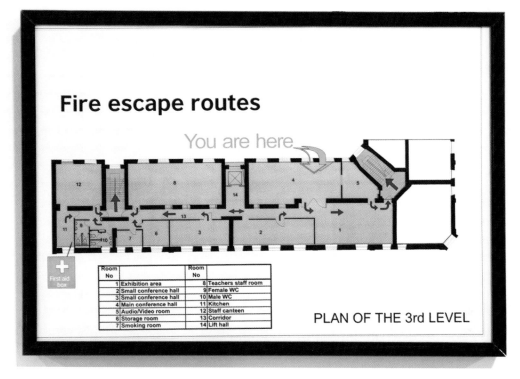

It is important to familiarise yourself with the fire escape routes in your workplace.

If you work for an organisation, the evacuation routes in your work setting should:

- be suitable for the people using them;

- be as short as possible and lead directly to an exit route;

- be sufficient in number for the people who will need to use them;

- be kept clear of obstructions at all times;

- be well maintained and immediately usable e.g. no damaged floors that might cause people to stumble, wet floors and spillages to be dealt with at once;

- be well lit by normal or emergency escape lighting;

- be wide enough for the number of people using the route, including wheelchair users and people with other mobility equipment;

- have doors that open in the direction of travel, if possible, and be quick and easy to open without a key;

- never be close to sources of fuel or other ignition risks;

- be accessible to the emergency services.

The regulatory bodies will take account of all the points made above when they are registering and inspecting health and social care settings.

The evacuation of buildings can present a considerable challenge in many health and social care settings, particularly those which are residential and provide support to a number of people with impaired mobility or other additional impairments, and where it is difficult for people to escape quickly and immediately to a place of total safety in the open air (usually called single stage evacuation). In such situations, it is recommended that services develop a strategy of progressive horizontal evacuation as described below:

> The process of horizontal evacuation relies on the parts of the building that are used for sleeping accommodation being separated into smaller sub-compartments called protected areas. These are areas separated from each other on the same level by walls and doors that provide at least 30 minutes of fire resistance. Each protected area should have at least two alternative exits to adjoining areas.
>
> If a fire occurs, residents can be moved away from the affected area to the adjoining protected area, where they are able to remain for a time in reasonable safety.
>
> *From: Fire Safety Risk Assessment: Residential Care Premises* www.communities.gov.uk

Protected areas can also be provided in services other than residential services. Any evacuation of people to protected areas or temporary 'places of refuge' should be included in consultation with local fire and rescue services and be clearly detailed in fire control plans. As a support worker you must be informed about the use of such alternative evacuation procedures and trained in how to use them. Fire and rescue services attending a fire must be fully informed about their use.

Further information about evacuation procedures is available from the following websites and from the reference materials at the end of this chapter:

- www.nashics.org
- www.nifrs.org
- www.communities.gov.uk

Evacuation procedures in community settings

It is also important for you to know about fire evacuation procedures in public buildings, since at least some of your support work is likely to take place out in community settings, for example when shopping, undertaking leisure activities and voluntary work. Here are some of the things you might need to know about:

- Public lifts and stair lifts cannot be used if there is a fire.

- Many public buildings have a 'place of refuge' or 'a place of reasonable safety' which can be used by disabled people and others who have mobility or other impairments which make it difficult to get out of the building. The refuge should be sufficiently protected or remote from the fire risk; it could be in a corridor, part of a public area or stairway, an open space such as a balcony, etc. There should be procedures in place to evacuate people from this area to a permanent place of safety – this could be by using a self-contained stairwell as a temporary refuge area and then moving the person/s down the stairs using evacuation chairs to a pre-arranged assembly point outside the building.

- The use of refuge areas should be part of the fire risk assessment for the building and procedures should be discussed with staff and any training needs identified, in particular the use of equipment such as evacuation chairs.

- A suitably trained member of staff should accompany and stay with the disabled person in the place of refuge, and evacuation should take place as soon as possible.

- Any specialist evacuation equipment required should be immediately accessible, e.g. evacuation chairs.

- The dignity and confidence of the person needs to be taken into account as part of the planning of evacuation procedures.

- The evacuation process for disabled persons should be regularly practised as part of fire drills.

Personal Emergency Evacuation Plans

Another thing you might come across in relation to public buildings is something called a Personal Emergency Evacuation Plan (PEEP). In situations where the person you support uses a particular building regularly, when doing voluntary or paid work, for example, their needs should be discussed with them and it may be decided that they require a PEEP. PEEPs are based on the need to consult with disabled employees and take into account the different features of the building. The PEEP specifies how the disabled person will be alerted to an emergency situation and then how he or she will reach safety.

PEEPs are not intended for settings in which the specific purpose is to provide health and social care, as the individual needs of all people are taken into account in the fire safety measures developed specifically by and for those services.

Fire escape routes in someone's home

The information above applies to organisations and/or to public buildings, but what about clear evacuation routes if you work in someone's home? If you are employed by an organisation to provide support in someone's home, they should have clear guidance on escape routes as part of their fire safety and training. However, the picture is less clear if your employer is the person you support, or his or her relative. In this case, fire safety, as mentioned earlier in this chapter, is a crucial element of agreed ways of working.

There are no clearly defined requirements, apart from the fact that the person employing you has responsibility for your health and safety. There is information on the government website listed previously in this chapter.

Here is their advice.

- Make an escape plan, explain it to everyone in the household and practise it. The best escape route is often the normal way in and out of your home.

- Think of any difficulties you may have getting out, e.g. at night you may need to have a torch to light your way; you might need equipment for a disabled person, such as a Zimmer frame or wheelchair.

- Choose a second escape route, in case the first one is blocked.

- Keep all exits clear of obstructions.

- If you can't escape, you'll need to find a room to take refuge in. This is especially important if you have difficulty moving around or going downstairs on your own. Choose a room with a window. Think about which room might be best for this – you need a window that can be opened and, if possible, a phone for calling 999.

- If you can, put cushions, towels or bedding at the bottom of the door to block smoke.

- Decide where the keys to doors and windows should be kept and always keep them there. Make sure everyone in the household knows where they are.

- Put a reminder of what to do in a fire somewhere where it will be seen regularly, like on the fridge door.

- Put your address by the phone so that it can be read out to the emergency services.

- Practise the plan and regularly remind everyone what to do and what not to do if a fire occurs.

This information can provide you with some useful starting points for discussion with the person you support, or a family carer, and/or a checklist in relation to escape plans in the event of a fire. As an employee, you share responsibility with your employer for the safety of everyone involved. The fire safety and escape plans must take account of the particular circumstances in which the person lives, including the number of people in the house, the mobility and capacity of the person/s concerned, the type of accommodation, whether it is a house or flat, the number of people likely to be available to help. Fire safety officers in your locality are the best people to offer advice so it's a good idea to make sure you know where to contact them.

In planning for, or responding to, any emergency, it's important to strike the balance between informing and preparing people and avoiding alarming them. Some people with learning disabilities have particularly high levels of anxiety, or difficulties absorbing information or understanding how it relates to their current situation. For example, discussion about fire safety might make someone think there is a fire at that moment, or make them unduly fearful. You know the person/s you support, so you will be in the best position to reassure them in the right way.

Why maintaining clear evacuation routes is important

It is important to maintain clear evacuation routes for the following reasons:

- to enable everyone to escape from the premises as quickly and safely as possible;

- because the people you support may be particularly at risk on account of mobility limitations, their capacity to understand and/or respond, their level of fear or anxiety and the amount of support they require;

- because badly maintained evacuation routes can hinder evacuation and put people at even greater risk;

- to demonstrate to people with a learning disability how to keep evacuation routes clear and encourage them to get into the habit of reporting any hazards or obstacles.

Bearing in mind the information you have just read in this chapter, think about your own work situation and answer the following questions:

- *In your own work setting, why is it important to maintain clear evacuation routes (escape routes in a house) in the event of a fire? Give as many reasons as you can and consider:*
  - *(i) the type of setting you work in;*
  - *(ii) the capacity and needs of the person/s you support.*
- *What is your own role in maintaining clear evacuation/escape routes and helping those you support to understand the importance of maintaining clear routes?*

Key points from this chapter

- You can prevent fires starting or spreading by:
  - ensuring that you are fully informed about fire safety policies and procedures and/or agreed ways of working and following these explicitly;
  - helping the person/s you support understand ways of preventing fires;
  - knowing where to access and how to use fire fighting equipment.
- You need to be clear about emergency procedures in the event of a fire, including:
  - how to raise the alarm;
  - procedures for contacting the emergency services;
  - where the fire assembly points are (in an organisation);
  - how to help people move away from the danger area.
- Clear evacuation or escape routes must be maintained at all times to enable people to escape quickly. This is particularly important when people have impaired mobility, difficulties in understanding or other needs that might affect evacuation.

References and where to go for more information

References

Department for Communities and Local Government (2012) *Fire and Emergencies.* www.communities.gov.uk

Department for Communities and Local Government (2006) *Fire Safety Risk Assessment Residential Care Premises.* www.communities.gov.uk

Department for Communities and Local Government (2007) *Fire Safety Risk Assessment – Means of Escape for Disabled People (Supplementary Guide).* www.communities.gov.uk

Directgov (2012) *Fire Safety in the Home.* www.direct.gov.uk

HM Government (2006) *Fire Safety Risk Assessment Residential Care Premises.* www.communities.gov.uk

National Association for Safety and Health in Care Services and Chief Fire Officers Association (CFOA) Enforcement Working Group (Valid from January 2011– January 2014) *Additional Guidance for Application to HM Government Guide to Fire Safety Risk Assessment Residential Care Premises Good Practice Guidance.* www.nashics.org

Websites

Department for Communities and Local Government www.communities.gov.uk

National Association for Safety and Health in Care Services www.nashics.org

Northern Ireland Fire and Rescue Service www.nifrs.org

Chapter 10

Security measures in the work setting

Oakwood Lodge is a residential home for people with learning disabilities that is divided into four different houses. It has security measures for access into the building and between the different houses that include a signing in and out book for staff and one for visitors, a coded entry system at the front door and between the different houses. It has become practice for residents' relatives to be given the code for the front door rather than having to ring for entry, in order, the manager says, to make the place friendlier and more accessible to people's families. Relatives quite often pass on the codes to other people seeking entry, assuming that they are also people's families.

Introduction

In the story above, you can see the logic in giving families the code, can't you, but you can also see how this could endanger security.

Like other aspects of health and safety, security in the work setting is a responsibility shared by the employer and the employee. This chapter explores the importance of security in the work setting and how it can be managed. Security covers the protection of people, premises, property and information.

Learning outcomes

This chapter will help you to:

- understand and demonstrate measures that are designed to protect your own security at work and the security of those you support;

- learn and demonstrate agreed measures for checking the identity of anyone requesting access to premises or information;

- explain the importance of ensuring that others are aware of your own whereabouts.

This chapter covers:

Common Induction Standards – Standard 8 – Health and safety in an adult social care setting: Learning Outcome 9

Level 2 HSC 027 – Contribute to health and safety in health and social care: Learning Outcome 8

Level 3 HSC 037 – Promote and implement health and safety in health and social care: Learning Outcome 8

Measures to protect security in the work setting

Given that people with learning disabilities are supported in an ever increasing range of services, as discussed previously in this book, we would expect security measures to differ according to the setting, although the basic principles are the same. In nursing or residential homes, it can be a challenge to create a homely setting while still preserving security. In a person's own home, it can be difficult to balance security and the person's rights to his or her own choice of lifestyle.

Security is governed by the Health and Safety at Work Act 1974. The bodies which regulate the quality of care also oversee security in health and social care settings (the Care Quality Commission, England; the Scottish Commission for the Regulation of Social Care; the Care Standards Inspectorate for Wales; the Regulation and Quality Improvement Authority, Northern Ireland).

Protecting people includes, amongst other things, safeguarding them from abuse and neglect. Because abuse and neglect are such significant issues, there are separate induction and qualification units allocated to these topics, so they are not covered in this book. You will know from your induction and any subsequent training you have done that you must report immediately any abuse you see or suspect.

You can find out more about safeguarding and protection issues in the book by Simon Bickerton (2011) *Principles of Safeguarding and Protection for Learning Disability Workers* in this series.

Your employer's responsibilities for security in the work setting

From reading previous chapters, you will know that your employer has a responsibility to ensure that your work setting is a safe place for employees, the people who use the service and others on the premises, such as visitors. This includes:

- consulting employees on security issues (usually done through a health and safety representative);
- assessing risks to security (of people, premises, property and information);
- giving all employees information about the security risks in your workplace;
- telling everyone about protection measures;
- instructing and training employees on how to deal with the risks. (In an organisation such as a day centre, residential or nursing home, or short breaks service, this information will be in the workplace policies and procedures, and you have a responsibility to ensure you are familiar with these and follow them as specified.)

Your responsibilities for security in the work setting

You have a responsibility to cooperate with your employer in ensuring your own safety and security and that of everyone else associated with your work setting.

In an organisation

In an organisation, you must:

- cooperate with your employer, ensure you are familiar with policies and procedures which set out security measures and systems for your work setting and follow these rigorously;

- contribute to risk assessments on security factors as required;

- report any security breaches or concerns to your line manager or other appropriate person;

- enable the people you support to understand and comply with and use required security measures as much as they are able to;

- report any incidents, breaches of security or other concerns you might have.

These responsibilities and your duty of care to the person/s you support require you to take all reasonable precautions to ensure his or her safety and security.

In someone's own home

If you're employed by an organisation, your own security and that of the person you support will be one of the issues dealt with in your induction and ongoing training. You will probably have information about being a 'lone worker', something which is dealt with towards the end of this chapter.

However you are employed, you have the same responsibility for your own security, that of the person you support and anyone else affected by your work. It's *how* things are done to ensure security that is different, as you would expect. Wearing name badges, for instance, is not appropriate in someone's home, but might be deemed a suitable security measure in a large nursing home.

Another difference is in how you agree and record security measures. You obviously wouldn't have formal written policies and procedures, but you would probably talk about relevant security issues together and agree ways of dealing with them. This might include locking the front door and not opening the door to people you don't know.

Some of this might be in the person's support plan, especially if there are clearly identifiable serious risks. For example, someone who has challenging behaviours and who might endanger him or herself or other people; someone who is very trusting and lets strangers in regularly; someone who has a very high anxiety level; someone involved in the criminal justice system.

Louise is helping Victoria to do her shopping and they are in the supermarket in the centre of the town. 'I'll leave you here,' she says to Victoria, 'I'm just popping in to the chemist to get a couple of things.'

Is Louise being negligent? Is she failing in her duty of care and putting Victoria's safety and security at risk? What do you think?

Well, it depends. You could say yes – Louise is there to be with Victoria, not to do things for herself that she ought to be doing in her own time. But ... supposing this is part of a phased process, outlined in Victoria's support plan, to help her become more confident in doing her own shopping? Maybe it's something she and Louise have planned together. If it is, they should have taken account of relevant factors. For example, does Victoria feel ready now to do this on her own? What are the risks to her security? Does she know what to do if anything goes wrong? And so on.

People with a learning disability and their responsibilities for security in the work setting

People with a learning disability who are using the service also have a duty to look after their own safety and security and that of those who support them. The extent to which they have the capacity to do this will of course vary considerably from person to person. You have an obligation to help them to understand their responsibilities, protect themselves and avoid putting anyone else at risk. How you do this depends on the type of work setting and the capacity and needs of the person or people you support. This is explored later.

Security measures in an organisation

Security measures in an organisation might include some or all of the following.

- Giving certain employees responsibility for particular aspects of security.
- Having security systems, e.g. security lights, locks, alarms, door entry phones. These must be well maintained and checked regularly.
- Coded doors or swipe cards for entry to the building and different areas.
- Identity badges for staff with names, photographs and the person's position – this is more likely to be used in certain health care settings such as nursing homes.

- Signing in/out books for staff.

- Signing in/out books for visitors.

- Clear policies and procedures about security with checklists where relevant.

- Ensuring that all employees know the security procedures and follow them rigorously, including what to do if there's an intruder.

- Presenting security information in an accessible way for people using the service; for instance, easy read leaflets about keeping safe.

- 'Property books' or files to record people's belongings.

- Procedures and formats to report breaches of security and action taken.

- Complaints procedures relating to security (this might be part of general complaints procedures).

Locked doors and deprivation of liberty

An issue you might come across when dealing with security is the question of the balance between a person's rights, security and safety in terms of 'deprivation of liberty'. This is more likely to be relevant in an organisation rather than in someone's own home. For example, in a large building, it might make sense to have locked doors between different areas and to restrict access to authorised staff. Vulnerable people who are unaware of danger might be better protected if doors are locked and they are prevented from wandering. In services which provide for people with challenging behaviours, locked doors might also be a security feature. But locked doors can also mean that the people being supported by the service are being deprived of their liberty.

The Mental Capacity Act Deprivation of Liberty Safeguards (England and Wales) and the Code of Practice for Local Authorities exercising functions under the Adults with Incapacity Act (Scotland) provide guidance on the tensions between rights, protection and safeguarding liberty in health and social care settings. (In Northern Ireland a new Mental Capacity Act has been prepared and is undergoing discussion at the time of writing this publication.)

You do not need to have detailed knowledge of this legislation, but you do need to be aware of the implications of locked doors and the restrictions to liberty these might cause. If you have any concerns or questions, you need to discuss them with your employer.

Security measures in someone's own home

It can be both easier and more difficult to ensure security when you are supporting someone in their own home. Easier because you usually have only one person to consider, but more difficult because you have to balance the person's rights against his or her security needs.

> Michael, who lives in a ground floor flat, leaves all his windows wide open in the summer, even when he's sleeping, because he likes fresh air and says the flat gets too warm. Anna, one of his support workers, worries about this in case the open windows attract an intruder.
>
> Sean goes to the local pub most nights and talks to everyone he meets. He often invites people back to his flat afterwards.
>
> Isabel often goes out and forgets to lock her front door. When at home, she always leaves the keys in the lock because her mother did this in case there was a fire and she had to get out quickly.

These situations, and many others, can cause dilemmas for support workers. You need to help people recognise the possible consequences of their actions, but you have no right to dictate what they do in their own homes. It is highly probable that other workers will have experienced similar situations, so discussing ways of dealing with such situations, especially ones that have worked in practice, will be helpful.

Activity

Think about as many things as possible that 'security' and 'security measures' could mean in your own work setting.

What are the challenges and how might you overcome them?

Discuss your ideas with a senior colleague or your line manager. If you are employed by the person you support, or a family carer, discuss these points with them as appropriate.

How did you get on? Once you have read the whole of this chapter, you might like to come back to this activity and see if you want to add anything.

In carrying out your responsibilities you will probably do some or all of the following:

- Discuss with the person you support, or a family carer if this is appropriate, the need for, and ways of preserving, security and presenting information in suitably accessible ways. You could use home safety leaflets from your local library, easy read materials, etc.

- Make use of any local schemes for vulnerable people – this might include a visit from a crime prevention officer (details from the local council or police).

- Encourage the person to:

  - make sure doors and windows are securely locked when they go out;

  - check people's identities before letting them into the house;

  - fit an intruder alarm;

  - have a chain and peephole on the front door;

  - avoid leaving keys in the lock or near the door;

  - have a security light;

  - keep valuables out of sight;

  - avoid having keys labelled with name or address;

When you support a person in their own home, it is the person who should be answering the door and phone, with support if they need it.

- dispose of personal information (e.g. bank statements) safely by shredding or tearing up into very small pieces;

- avoid letting strangers into their home.

- You might also want to talk about having safety reminders posted on the fridge or kitchen notice board and help them prepare these.

The website www.suzylamplugh.org has useful factsheets and other information about personal safety at home, so you might like to have a look at the ones that are relevant to your work. You might also find the following easy read leaflets helpful for the person you support.

Making sure you are safe – easy read leaflet from www.camden.gov.uk

Keeping you safe – easy read leaflet from www.coventry.gov.uk

Safety when out in the community

Some or all of your support work might take place outside the person's home, in different community settings. If you are with the person, you will know how to keep yourself and the person safe. You will have had discussions and possibly training about this. But what about the person's security when you are not with them?

There are some general safety guidelines you can discuss with the person, some of which they will probably be aware of. For example:

- knowing bus and train routes and what to do if they encounter problems, especially at night, e.g. if the bus doesn't turn up;

- having their mobile phone with them at all times and knowing who to contact for help;

- keeping money and valuables out of sight;

- not talking to strangers;

- not going off with anyone they don't know;

- if out alone at night, staying in well lit places where there are people around;

- sitting near the driver if the bus is almost empty;

- staying with friends and not going off by themselves, especially if they are out at night;

- making sure someone knows where they are going, especially at night;

- never accepting lifts from strangers no matter how friendly;
- ordering taxis from companies they know.

There are general safety guidelines that you can discuss with the person you support, such as having a plan of what to do if a bus doesn't turn up.

There's a fine line between respecting the person's rights and adulthood and helping them to stay safe. If you have a good and trusting relationship with the person, as you should, you will know how to strike the balance.

Activity

The 'What if...?' discussion is a useful one to have with the person you support, e.g. 'What if the bus breaks down?', 'What if you get lost?', 'What if you lose your money?' It can be quite light-hearted but with a serious purpose and you can take turns at asking one another, which can help the person challenge you, but also enables him or her to think through the problems they might have to face.

Think about someone you support and prepare a list of 'What if...?' questions. Explain the activity to them and ask them some questions. Wait for the answers. Then tell them some of the situations in which you have to be careful about security and ask them to make up some 'What if...?' questions for you (with help if necessary).

You can repeat this activity at intervals to reinforce security measures.

If the person you support has profound and multiple learning disabilities, you could use the activity with a colleague or the person's relative if appropriate. It might help you think through other security measures.

Personal security and people with challenging behaviours

People with challenging behaviours can put themselves and others at risk without understanding what they are doing. So it is extremely important that risk assessments take their needs into account and that support workers and the people themselves, as far as they can understand, have workable strategies for preventing and dealing with situations which might present danger. These will be in the person's support plan. If you work in a service which caters specifically for people with challenging behaviours, you will receive in-depth training about keeping yourself and other people safe. If your service is a generic one and you regularly support someone with challenging behaviours, you should receive appropriate training. If you haven't yet done so, you should talk to your line manager or other appropriate person.

You can find out more about supporting a person whose behaviour may challenge in the book by Sharon Paley in this series (2012) *Promoting Positive Behaviour for People with a Learning Disability and People with Autism*.

Checking the identity of anyone requesting access to premises or information

An important aspect of security in the work setting is to make sure people seeking access to premises, people and information have a right to obtain access.

In an organisation

In a busy workplace it can be difficult to keep track of who is where and doing what, especially when there is an open door policy for visiting. If you see people you don't recognise you can't be sure whether they are relatives or friends of a person who uses the service, visiting professionals such as doctors, contractors, or people who have no right to be there and who present a security risk.

Organisations will have systems in place to check the identity of anyone who requests access to the premises, people or information, as discussed in the previous section. If you do come across someone you don't recognise, you should always check their identity. It's usually enough to say, 'Can I help you?'

- Don't be put off if they say no. Ask them directly who they are and who they've come to see. Genuine visitors won't mind – they'll be pleased to know you're security conscious.

- If their answer appears genuine, don't just let them continue on their way. Say, 'I'll show you where (the person) is,' or, 'I'll take you there.'

- If the person says they're here for a work-related purpose, e.g. to mend or collect something, ask for ID.

- If you have any concerns, ask the person to go with you to see the person in charge or another senior colleague, and ask for advice.

In addition:

- Never let someone you don't know into the building without checking their photographic identification if they say they are a contractor or visiting professional. Check with your line manager if the person claims to be a relative or friend of a person who uses the service.

- Never give anyone access codes without authorisation from a manager.

Access to information

Security is also about protecting information so that it is available only to people who have the right to access it. For example, a person's GP would have access to his or her medical record whereas a relative or friend would not without the permission of the person concerned. Personal and private information in a service is protected by the Data Protection Act 1998 and should never be made available without the individual's permission or that of the main carer if the person is judged not to have the capacity to consent. You can learn more about the Data Protection Act, the Mental Capacity Act (England and Wales) and the Adults with Incapacity Act (Scotland) at:

- www.legislation.gov.uk

- www.justice.gov.uk

- www.scotland.gov.uk

As a general rule:

- Always check the identity of the person asking for the information, both on the phone and in person;

- Do not give out information that the person concerned has not agreed to disclose;

- If cleared to do so, give out only information requested, nothing additional;

- If in doubt, seek guidance from your line manager or other senior colleague.

There may be times, however, when it can be difficult to know whether you are permitted to pass on information or not, especially if the person is unable to consent, has no known relatives or is very ill. In all such circumstances you should be guided by the policies in your work setting and advice from your line manager.

You can find out more about what actions to take if you are concerned about the security of information in the book by Lesley Barcham and Jackie Pountney, *Handling Information for a Learning Disability Worker* (2011) that is part of this series.

Thinking point

Simon has been diagnosed with bowel cancer and his family doesn't want him to know as they think he wouldn't be able to fully understand and would be very frightened. The doctor isn't happy about this situation but Simon's mother is adamant that he shouldn't know. Krish, the manager of the residential home, with Simon's mother's permission, tells Tom, his named support worker.

Krish thinks Simon has a right to know, but Tom agrees with his mother that it's better for him not to be told.

Who is right? Should other staff be told? Who could people get advice from in this situation?

If you've ever been in a situation similar to this where information is being kept from the person concerned, for the very best of reasons, you'll understand how complex it is. It isn't a question of who is right or wrong. It's about who has the right to decide whether Simon should know or not. It's likely that there will be ongoing, and very sensitive, discussion with Simon's mother, involving the doctor and Krish. Simon's rights and wellbeing will be paramount in this process.

Restricting access for relatives and friends

One of the difficulties you might encounter is what to do when someone you support does not want to see particular relatives or friends. This can be difficult to deal with, but obviously it is the person's right to refuse to see anyone they don't wish to see.

Stevie lives in a residential home for people with learning disabilities. His sister visits regularly and his two brothers occasionally. Staff have noticed that Stevie seems upset after visits from his older brother, Mark. Stevie has communication difficulties, but on the last occasion Mark visited he made it clear that he didn't want to see him. Marion, Stevie's key worker, is pretty sure that this is because Mark teases Stevie about his interests, tells him to 'act like a man' and looks through his possessions without asking. Marion has told Mark that Stevie doesn't want to see him and Mark, who is upset and angry, says they have no right to keep him from seeing his brother.

It isn't easy to work out a solution in this difficult situation without knowing the people concerned and having more information, but whatever happens, the first responsibility of the service is to Stevie.

There might also be a need to restrict visitors when someone is too ill to see anyone, for example in a nursing home. If this is relevant to you, you should make sure you are clear about your organisation's procedures on how this is to be managed.

In the home setting

These guidelines are fine for an organisation, but what if your support work takes place in someone's home? Security is no less important there, and sometimes more so since there might not be anyone else around to assist if anything goes wrong.

Our personalities and experiences shape who we are – more trusting or more suspicious, overly anxious or pretty relaxed, and so on. People with learning disabilities who are particularly trusting, anxious or fearful, may have additional reasons why they are like this. Perhaps they have only limited experience of living in their own homes, or maybe they've been exploited, bullied or abused previously. They might have difficulty with communication, or of understanding what is going on in a situation. All of this makes them more vulnerable to bogus callers, most of whom are very skilled in what they do. Most people who live in their own homes, whether alone or with a partner or flatmate, will have had the opportunity to discuss the issue of who to let into their house. So security in the home is a vitally important element of your support work and something you should make sure you give time to.

Some of the home security measures discussed earlier, such as door chains, spy holes, entry phones and keeping the door locked are useful ways of keeping out unwanted callers. You should also impress upon the person:

- their right to decide who they have in their own home;

- never to let anyone in if they don't know them;

- to tell you and their other support workers about any anxieties they have about this and about anyone who has been to their door whom they're not sure of; a friendly neighbour can also be helpful in this instance, but only if the person and you are sure about them.

If a stranger comes to the door when you are there, don't take over – let the person answer the door and support them in asking for ID or refusing entry. Obviously if the person has a particular reason for asking you to deal with the caller, e.g. they are ill or not wanting to see someone, that's a different matter.

Many utilities companies, such as gas and electricity, have password schemes for elderly people and other people classed as vulnerable, so this is something that might be useful to the person you support. There is a lot of information on the internet about how password schemes work so you might like to check out your local area or the utility companies used by the person you support.

The importance of ensuring that others are aware of your own whereabouts

Clearly your own security is important to you and you wouldn't want to do anything that puts you at risk. You need to know how to safeguard yourself and others in your day-to-day work, but there may also be situations where you need to be particularly careful – working on your own, for instance, at night or in early mornings, in isolated places or in settings which present particular difficulties. Letting other people know about your whereabouts is an important security precaution.

As mentioned earlier in this chapter, your employer has a duty to provide you with personal safety and security information. This is particularly relevant in situations which present greater risk. For instance:

- where you work alone in the community;

- where you work in a large building with extensive grounds, especially if you have night duties;

- in some situations where you support people who have challenging behaviours.

In the community

If you work alone in the community or make home visits as part of your work, your employer should have in place a 'lone worker' policy that provides information and guidance on safety and security. This will include the following:

- Procedures for providing information about home visits, such as where you are going and what time you intend to return. If all of your work takes place in the community, this information will be on your work rota, so you should report any changes to your line manager, for example if someone is taken ill and you have to accompany them to hospital; or if the person is not at home or you cannot get in.

- A list of any safety equipment required, e.g. a mobile phone, personal safety alarm.

- A risk assessment for each person being supported and their home, as there might be particular hazards in the home, e.g. an unfriendly dog, or the house is in a poor state of repair.

- A list of agreed procedures to follow if you feel unsafe in a situation.

- Regular supervision to allow you to discuss any personal safety issues which concern you or changes in circumstances.

You should discuss any personal safety concerns at your regular supervision.

In a residential setting

Employers will have carried out risk assessments and put in place procedures for dealing with situations that pose a danger – these might be for night workers, people working in isolated areas, etc. Make sure you are familiar with them. In addition:

- you should know how to raise the alarm if you are in a threatening situation;

- make sure your colleagues know where you are working, especially at night, even if this is just in an adjoining part of the building;

- try not to walk through the grounds on your own, especially at night, but if this cannot be avoided, a personal alarm might be useful.

Working with people with challenging behaviours

By no means do all people whose behaviour is seen as challenging present a safety risk to other people. This is more likely to happen when the person finds a situation frightening or threatening and feels in danger. If you work with someone with challenging behaviours, there should be clear procedures in place to show you how to defuse the situation. The extent to which these procedures are developed might depend on the setting. In a specialist setting where staff are trained particularly in supporting people with challenging behaviours, there will be greater expertise and knowledge. In other more generic settings, there may be a need to bring in specialist help.

Challenging behaviour is a complex issue and must be seen in the context of the needs and situation of the person concerned, e.g. the reason for the behaviour: previous life experiences – abuse for example; communication difficulties; fear of anything new or different; and so on. Guidelines for responding to challenging behaviours and keeping the person, yourself and other people safe should be in place as a result of an individual risk assessment.

You may be in a situation where you work alone with someone who has challenging behaviours, in a day or residential service, out in the community or in the person's home. You need to follow the same procedures outlined above and make sure that your whereabouts are known to your line manager, colleagues and/or other relevant people.

BILD has produced a wide range of resources to support people and organisations in developing their understanding and skills in adopting positive behaviour support approaches and reducing restrictive practices. You can get more information at www.bild.org.uk/our-services/positive-behaviour-support

Key points from this chapter

- Security measures in the work setting cover people, premises, property and information.

- Your employer has a responsibility for the security of all employees, people with a learning disability and relevant others. There should be clear policies and procedures dealing with security measures and all employees must be made aware of these.

- In someone's home security is no less important and you have a responsibility to protect your own safety and that of the person you support. This should be part of the ways of working agreed between you and the person you support, or a family carer if appropriate.

- You should always check the identity of anyone you don't recognise in the work setting to ensure they have a right to be there.

- If you support someone in their own home you need to help them to understand the importance of checking the identity of people seeking access to their house.

- Ensuring that other people know your own whereabouts at all times when you are working will help to safeguard your security.

References and where to go for more information

References

Barcham, L and Pountney, J (2011) *Handling Information for a Learning Disability Worker.* Exeter: BILD/Learning Matters

Bickerton, S (2011) *Principles of Safeguarding and Protection for Learning Disability Workers.* Exeter: BILD/Learning Matters

Camden Learning Disabilities Service (2012) *Making Sure you are Safe – Easy Read Leaflet.* www.camden.gov.uk

Coventry City Council (2005) *Keeping you Safe – Easy Read Leaflet.* www.coventry.gov.uk

Health and Safety Executive (HSE) (2012) *Violence in Health and Social Care.* www.hse.gov.uk/healthservices

Mencap (2009) *Consent and Decision-making: Financial Matters for People with a Learning Disability Aged 18 or Over.* www.mencap.org.uk

Paley, S (2012) *Promoting Positive Behaviour when Supporting People with a Learning Disability and People with Autism.* London: Sage/Learning Matters/ BILD

Social Care Institute for Excellence (SCIE) (2011) *At a glance 37: Challenging Behaviour: A Guide for Family Carers on Getting the Right Support for Adults.* www.scie.org.uk

West Mercia Police (2012) *How to Beat Distraction Burglars.* www.westmercia. police.uk

Legislation and reports

Data Protection Act 1998 www.legislation.gov.uk

Mental Capacity Act (2005) www.justice.gov.uk

Websites

BILD Positive Behaviour Support information www.bild.org.uk/our-services/ positive-behaviour-support

Live Life Safe Suzy Lamplugh Trust www.suzylamplugh.org

Chapter 11

Managing stress

Carol, a support worker in a residential home told me, 'I love my job. I wouldn't do anything else no matter what they paid me.' If you saw her at work you'd know this is true. She got on very well with all the people she supported and was always busy. But you'd also hear her say on more than one occasion, 'I'm stressed out.' Particularly at the end of a hard shift when they were short staffed and it was pouring with rain.

Sue, on the other hand, never appeared to be stressed. She was always smiling. She seemed to have more of a relaxed approach to her work and there was the suspicion that she wasn't working as hard as her colleagues – she always had a reason if she was questioned. But if you met her on the way out after her shift, she'd tell you about all the things she was finding difficult outside of work. Her face and her demeanour changed as she spoke.

Introduction

Stress can have both positive and negative consequences – the stress that comes from competitive sports for example, which can urge the person on to excel, or act as an obstacle. The focus in this chapter is negative stress in the work setting, how to recognise the signs of stress and how to manage stress.

Learning outcomes

This chapter will help you to:

* recognise common indicators of stress in yourself and others;

* describe signs that indicate stress in yourself;

* identify and analyse circumstances that tend to trigger stress;

* describe and compare strategies for managing stress.

Common signs and indicators of stress

We all have different levels of tolerance, different factors and circumstances that cause us to be stressed, different ways of showing stress and different ways of dealing with it, as illustrated by the example of Carol and Sue at the beginning of this chapter.

Support work is demanding and stress levels can be high. You need to know:

- how to recognise the signs of stress in yourself and in other people;
- how to manage your own stress;
- what support you can expect in your work setting;
- when to seek help if stress seems to be getting out of hand.

Stress affects us emotionally and physically and has an effect on our behaviour in everyday life.

Stress can make us feel:

- restless, angry, fearful, weepy, listless, sad, guilty, unappreciated, irritable or depressed;
- that we can't be bothered to do anything, that we're worthless;
- powerless and that whatever we do it won't make any difference anyway;
- stretched to the limit, with no time for everything we've got to do, not knowing where to start;
- uninterested in anything.

Physical signs of stress include:

- headaches;
- muscle tension;
- high blood pressure, strokes, heart attacks;
- digestive disorders;
- changes in immune systems, making us more susceptible to infections;
- stomach aches and diarrhoea;
- sweating or shivering;
- skin problems.

Stress can have a variety of effects on everyday life. For example:

- difficulty sleeping and relaxing;
- changes in eating patterns;
- decreased energy levels or restless behaviour;
- excessive worrying;
- blaming other people;

Stress can influence us physically and emotionally as well as affecting our everyday life.

- difficulty communicating;

- inability to enjoy anything;

- having trouble thinking clearly, remembering things, or making decisions;

- outbursts of anger.

Some people seem able to withstand huge amounts of pressure and others seem to buckle at the slightest thing. In general though, the more serious the incident or event, the higher the level of stress, always allowing for individual differences.

Circumstances that can cause you stress

The main focus in this chapter is stress in the work setting. However, it is impossible to separate your work life and outside life completely, no matter how hard you try. If you are having difficulties with life outside work, e.g. problems with money or a relationship, an illness in someone you love or a bereavement, you can't just leave that aside. The effects of stress and ways of managing it are the same, no matter the cause of the stress, but the level of the stress and how often you experience it, as well as your ability to withstand stress, will have a bearing on how it affects you. For example, a trying day at work may leave you feeling exhausted, without an appetite and irritable. But going through a divorce *and* trying to cope with an unsupportive line manager will have more serious and longer lasting effects.

Here are some of the things that can trigger stress at work:

- not being clear about your own role and what is expected of you;

- your own workload;

- shortage of resources;

- staff shortages;

- fear of redundancy;

- lack of support from colleagues and/or managers, especially when you are stressed by things outside work;

- anxiety or worry about a person you support;

- dealing with difficult circumstances, such as the death of someone you support;

- some aspects of the type of work involved, especially the less pleasant parts;

- feeling under-valued;

- lack of opportunity for promotion and increase in salary.

Activity

Write down two things that cause you stress at work. How do these things affect you physically, emotionally and mentally?

Why do you think these things cause you stress? Think about:

- *Is any person or people involved in causing you this stress? How do you feel about them?*
- *The setting – are you alone, do you feel uncomfortable, at risk?*
- *Are you being asked to do something you don't like or feel able to do?*
- *Do you feel you are not getting enough support?*
- *Does the situation remind you about something painful outside work?*
- *Is your life outside work difficult at present?*
- *Can you think of other reasons why these things cause you stress?*

Who do you talk to for support? How does this help and why have you chosen this person to talk to?

Recognising stress in other people

It's said that we can best understand other people's troubles when we have gone through the same thing ourselves, but this is not always true. It can be really annoying to start telling a friend about something that's causing you stress only to have them break in as soon as the words are out of your mouth and say 'I know – I've been through it myself,' and then launch into their own worries, when all you want is for the person to *listen*. So it's important to be aware how to recognise when other people are stressed and how to support them.

Personality differences and personal experience come into play here. Some people are talkers, others are not and some are in the middle. Recognising stress in others isn't always easy. In the talker, how do you tell the difference between his or her everyday stress levels and something more serious? The same with someone who is naturally quiet – how do you know if something more stressful is happening? Giving and getting support as colleagues is an important aspect of managing stress at work. But what about the people with a learning disability you support, especially those who don't communicate in words or whose ability to speak is limited?

> Ayesha lives with her family, but has recently started spending time at Greenfields House once a month as part of her plan to move into her own home. She has profound and multiple learning disability and needs high levels of support with all her personal needs. She is generally very quiet, but cries every time her mother leaves her and this goes on for some time. She also cries every time any of the support workers come near her. Everyone is just getting to know her so they're hoping she'll settle and come to trust them.

We might not think of this as stress, just as Ayesha missing her mother. But she is clearly stressed, probably fearful, anxious, confused and a host of other things. She might not sleep or eat well. Because of their experience, this probably won't be anything new to the staff of the unit. They should have ways of managing it which will enable Ayesha to be less stressed and more secure and her mother to be less stressed and confident in the ability of staff to look after her daughter well.

Recognising stress in the person you work with is an important part of your support. You and others may not think of it as stress, just as the person being difficult or having a bad day. But if you relate it to your own feelings of stress, you can see certain behaviours indicate that the person is under pressure and feeling stressed. The signs of stress can be more extreme if the person doesn't communicate in words, like Ayesha.

Some people who have communication difficulties will become withdrawn when stressed, or upset, while others will react to stress by showing behaviour that is seen as challenging, as Thurman (2011) points out:

If you are anxious and the world feels like a very threatening and unpredictable place or you can't get your message across to others, it is likely that you might find other ways of expressing yourself, for example:

- grabbing things (instead of asking);
- pushing (instead of waiting or saying *excuse me*);
- hitting (instead of saying *please don't do that*);
- screaming (instead of asking *can we do something different now?*).

It is helpful to ask yourself if there are hidden messages when somebody behaves in such ways rather than simply labelling them as 'challenging' (Thurman, 2011).

Can you imagine the level of stress you would experience if you were unable to communicate what you felt, thought, needed or wanted? It's stressful enough in a country where you don't speak the language.

Thinking about challenging behaviours as stress can help us to understand them better, identify the cause of the stress and remove or reduce the trigger.

Thinking point

Think about one person you support and the different ways he or she shows stress. If the person doesn't talk, how do you know he or she is stressed?

Strategies for managing stress

As we know, the level, frequency and duration of stress is important in helping you decide what to do about it. If your stress is occasional and the effects not too severe, even though unpleasant, it is easier to manage than continual severe stress which leaves you seriously debilitated. In both cases, the answer is to take action rather than just let it go on. Even fairly minor stressful situations can wear you down if they go on for a long time.

You will feel better if you take control and deal with stress actively and positively. Here are some strategies that people find useful for dealing with stress.

- Doing something active, like going for a walk, swimming, gardening or playing a sport – channelling your energy into something different can help relieve stress.

- Taking part in a leisure activity, such as the cinema, theatre, a drink at the pub, knitting or craft work – again you're using your energy in a positive way.

Taking part in a leisure activity can help you to manage your stress.

- Learning relaxation techniques and using them when you are in a stressful situation and also to unwind afterwards.

- Complementary therapies help some people, such as massage, hypnotherapy, reiki, yoga, and reflexology.

- Talking to someone who will *listen* – a friend or colleague inside or outside work.

- Discussing the situation with your line manager or other senior colleague who can help to resolve the problem and perhaps help you get new insight into the situation.

- Attending a stress management course.

- Taking more time for yourself.

- Writing things down – putting something on paper can sometimes help you offload and help you see ways of dealing with the situation; some people find that keeping a 'stress diary' can help them understand and manage stress better.

- Setting your boundaries – this is about asserting yourself positively, but politely and not just putting up with things that stress you. You might try explaining to someone who is always late on shift how this affects you – not an easy thing to do if you are not normally assertive, but it does help reduce stress levels and can help people change the way they do things.

- Thinking positively – if your stress is caused by thinking you can't do something, or aren't adequate, you *can* change your thinking and begin to believe in yourself. Every time you think negatively you are sending yourself a message which will reinforce your negative feelings. Instead, turn away from the negative thought and tell yourself something positive. It takes practice, but you can do it. Visualisation can help – visualising yourself doing positive things and being congratulated, for example.

Managing severe stress

There are times of course when stress reaches such proportions that you need to do something more serious about it, like taking time off work, getting help from your doctor or even changing your job. In these circumstances, you need to discuss the situation with your employer at an early stage rather than letting it continue to the point where it affects you more drastically.

Your employer has obligations under the Health and Safety at Work Act 1974 to take reasonable steps to ensure your health and safety, and this includes minimising the risk of stress-related illness or injury to employees. You can read more about this on the Health and Safety Executive website at www.hse.gov.uk

Activity

Use this activity to help you think about the best way of managing your own stress.

First, write down three things that cause you stress (the trigger), e.g. having to clear up after a colleague.

Second, alongside each of the three things on your list note down two ways you could deal with this stressful situation.

Finally, choose one way that you think would work best for you and explain why.

If you think it is appropriate discuss this activity with a trusted colleague or friend.

Helping people with learning disabilities manage stress

Many of the strategies for managing stress are equally useful to the people you support. You may have to adapt them if the person has a more severe learning or physical disability.

Joe is key worker for Lewis who has profound and multiple learning disabilities, and who gets very stressed when people don't understand him. As his project when doing a course, Joe decided to try wheelchair ice skating because Lewis likes lots of activity around him. He discusses the idea with Lewis's dad who agrees. As well as loving the skating, Lewis became more relaxed both physically and emotionally.

Obviously this was done with full attention to health and safety regulations and with appropriately qualified instructors. There are increasingly more opportunities for people who use wheelchairs to participate in sporting activities with the right support and specially trained staff.

Activity

Think of someone you support and of how you might help this person manage stress. Do you already know some of the things they enjoy that help them relax and enjoy life? Are there other things you can think of that might help them manage their stress? Discuss your ideas with the person, or their family carer, if this is appropriate, or you could talk to the person's key worker.

Key points from this chapter

- Understanding the triggers for your own stress can help you start to deal with it.

- Stress affects us emotionally and physically and can have an effect on our behaviour in everyday life.

- Recognising the signs of stress in others, including the person you support, and listening to them ('listening' involves listening to their behaviours and body language even if they don't communicate verbally) will help you support them more effectively.

- Don't let a stressful situation continue until it affects your health; get help and support and do something to ease the situation.

- There are tried and tested ways to manage stress; find some that suit you and use them.

References and where to go for more information

References

Health and Safety Executive (2007) *Managing the Causes of Work-Related Stress: A Step-by-Step Approach Using the Management Standards.* www.hse.gov.uk

Health and Safety Executive (HSE) (2012) *Work Related Stress.* www.hse.gov.uk

Royal College of Nursing (2005) *Managing Your Stress. A Guide for Nurses.* www.rcn.org.uk

Thurman, S (2011) *Communicating Effectively with People with a Learning Disability.* Exeter: Learning Matters/BILD

Websites

BILD Positive Behaviour Support information www.bild.org.uk/our-services/positive-behaviour-support/

Glossary

ABC – a first aid technique which stands for airway–breathing–circulation. It is the procedure used to assess someone's breathing and to help ensure that oxygen is supplied to the brain and vital organs while waiting for expert medical help to arrive.

Act (legal term) – a bill which has passed through the required legislative steps and has become law.

Agreed ways of working – a term developed in response to the diversity of ways support services are currently provided for people with a learning disability; it can be used to cover informal ways of working in someone's own home, but can also be applied to formal policies and procedures.

BME communities – people from black, Asian or other ethnic communities which are in the minority in the UK.

Braille – a system of reading and writing for blind and other sight impaired people.

Cardiac arrest – a cardiac arrest occurs when the heart stops pumping blood around the body.

Care and Social Services Inspectorate Wales – the body which regulates care services in Wales.

Care Inspectorate – the body which regulates social care services in Scotland.

Care Quality Commission – the independent regulator of health and social care services in England.

Challenging behaviour – behaviour which puts the safety of the person or others at risk or has a significant impact on the quality of life of the person or others.

Clinical waste – a term used to define waste which can be harmful to any person coming into contact with it and which may cause infection.

Code of conduct – a document provided by an organisation setting out the standards staff are expected to work to.

Code of practice – a document setting out the standards social care workers are expected to work to.

Control of Substances Hazardous to Health Regulations 2002 and Control of Substances Hazardous to Health (Amendment) Regulations 2003 (COSHH) – the legislation which sets out the procedures to be taken to prevent harm from the use of substances hazardous to health and safety.

Convulsive seizure – an epileptic seizure in which the person becomes unconscious, falls down and makes involuntary jerky movements.

Cross contamination – occurs when harmful bacteria is spread between food, substances or equipment.

Direct payments – a way for people to organise their own social care support by receiving funding from their local council following an assessment of their needs.

Duty of care – a professional responsibility to act in the best interest of the person receiving support or care.

Dysphagia – difficulties with eating, drinking or swallowing.

Epilepsy – recurrent seizures which are caused by a sudden burst of excess electrical activity in the brain, causing a temporary disruption in the normal message passing between brain cells.

Equality Act 2010 – the law which aims to protect the rights of disabled people and prevent disability discrimination.

European Regulation (EC) No 1272/2008 on classification, labelling and packaging (CLP) of substances and mixtures – the law which governs the labelling of hazardous substances.

Evacuation chair – a chair used to move people with impaired mobility out of danger areas in emergency situations such as fires.

Evacuation routes – planned routes to enable people to escape in emergency situations such as fires and which by law must form part of fire action plans in public buildings, work, health and social care settings.

Evacuation slide – a piece of equipment for moving people with impaired mobility down stairs in an emergency situation such as a fire.

Fire action plan – actions to be taken if a fire occurs in the work setting.

Fire Safety Regulations (Northern Ireland) 2010 – legislation governing fire safety in Northern Ireland.

Fire Scotland Act 2005 and Fire Safety (Scotland) Regulations 2006 – legislation governing fire safety in Scotland.

Food Safety Act 1990, amended by the Food Safety Act (Amendment) Regulations 2004 – legislation which sets out the general principles and requirements of food law in EU states.

Food Standards Agency – an independent Government department set up by an Act of Parliament in 2000 to protect the public's health and consumer interests in relation to food.

Hazard – a situation or event that has the potential to cause harm to people.

Hazardous substances and materials – substances and materials which create risk to people's health.

Health and Safety at Work Act 1974 – the key piece of legislation which governs health and safety in the work setting and which has given rise to additional laws about different areas of health and safety at work.

Health and Safety Executive – the national independent watchdog for work related health, safety and illness.

Health care tasks – tasks undertaken by health and social care workers which are related to a person's health care, e.g. dealing with catheter or stoma bags, changing dressings etc.

Healthcare Improvement Scotland – the body which regulates health care services in Scotland.

Healthcare Inspectorate Wales – the body which regulates health care services in Wales.

Hoist – a piece of equipment used to transfer people who are unable to move independently or to weight bear.

Horizontal progressive evacuation – a system of evacuation used when a fire has broken out and people cannot be evacuated quickly or easily to a place of total safety. Instead they are moved to a protected place which has walls and doors and which provides protection from fire for 30 to 60 minutes. They can then be moved to another protected place if it is not possible to move them immediately to a place of total safety away from the building.

Hydration – the availability of sufficient water in the human body.

Induction – a period of learning, shortly after starting a new job or volunteering placement, about how to provide good support to people with learning disabilities.

Infection – the invasion of disease into the human body.

Legislation – laws introduced by the government setting out people's rights and what is required to comply with these laws.

Lymphoedema – swelling that occurs as the result of an impaired lymphatic system.

Moving and positioning (sometimes called 'manual handling') – a term used to refer to situations in health and social care in which people with impaired mobility need support to move from one place to another. The term 'manual handling' is used more often nowadays to refer to moving equipment rather than people although training is still often called 'manual handling training'.

Nutrition – the provision of the foods we need to support life.

Personal Emergency Evacuation Plan (PEEP) – a term used in emergency situations such as fire and which details the procedures to be followed in order to enable someone with impaired mobility who requires assistance to escape from a building in an emergency situation.

Personal budget – a way of giving disabled people control over their own care and support by enabling them to employ their own support workers or allow a carer or advocate to do this on their behalf. Funding is allocated after an assessment of needs.

Person centred planning – a structured way to make sure that people with a learning disability are at the centre of all planning, choices and discussions about their life.

Personal assistant – someone employed directly by a person with a learning disability to provide care and support, usually through a direct payment or individual budget.

Place of temporary refuge – a safe place in a public building or work setting to which someone with impaired mobility can be moved to or moves to prior to being evacuated in the event of an emergency such as a fire.

Place of total safety – a place of evacuation in the event of a fire which is away from the fire and any danger.

Policy – a statement or plan of action that clearly sets out an organisation's position on, or approach to, a particular issue or aspect of work.

Postural care action group – a group of organisations which has launched a campaign to raise awareness of the importance of good postural care for thousands of people with multiple disabilities.

Procedure – a set of instructions that explains in detail how a policy should be put into practice and what staff should do in particular work situations relating to that policy.

Personal protective clothing and equipment – protective clothing such as gloves, aprons, masks and other equipment designed to act as a barrier and protect health and social care workers and those they support from infection or injury while undertaking tasks which might cause harm.

Rectal diazepam – medication for seizures which is administered rectally and used in emergency situations to stop cluster seizures.

Reporting of Injuries, Diseases and Dangerous Occurrences Regulation 1995 (RIDDOR) – legislation which sets out the circumstances and situations in which injuries, diseases and dangerous occurrences have to be reported.

Risk – the probability or threat of harm, injury or other negative occurrence which might be prevented through planned action.

Risk assessment – a careful examination of what could cause harm to people so that you can weigh up whether you have taken enough precautions or should do more to prevent any harm.

Routes to infection – the ways in which infection enters the human body.

Stand aid – a piece of equipment which is used to move people who cannot transfer independently but who can weight bear with assistance.

Stress – the feeling of being under too much mental or emotional pressure which affects the way in which we manage our day-to-day lives.

Index

A
ABC (airway–breathing–circulation) 41–2
accidents and sudden illness 33–49
  ecording and reporting 38–40
  types of 34
agreed ways of working 6–10

B
balanced diet 79–81
basic emergency techniques 40–8
  burns and scalds 47–8
  cardiac arrest 46
  choking 42–3
  dysphagia 43–4
  epilepsy 45–6
  loss of consciousness 44–5
  problems with breathing 41–2
  severe bleeding 46–7
  suspected fractures 47
black and minority ethnic communities, risk
      assessment and 27–8
bleeding 46–7
burns and scalds 47–8

C
cardiac arrest 46
cardiopulmonary resuscitation (CPR) 46
Care and Social Services Inspectorate Wales 6, 131
Care Inspectorate (Scotland) 6, 131
Care Quality Commission (CQC) 5–6, 131
care regulators 5–6
challenging behaviours
  security and 139, 145
  stress and 153–4
Chemicals (Hazard Information and Packaging for
      Supply) Regulations 2009 (CHIP) 103–4
choking 42–3
clinical waste 69–70
*Code of Practice on the Prevention and Control of
      Infections and Related Guidance* 63
Code of Practice for Local Authorities exercising
      functions under the Adults with Incapacity
      Act (Scotland) 134
coloured chopping boards 76
Control of Substances Hazardous to Health
      (Amendment) Regulations 2003 (COSHH)
      5, 101
Control of Substances Hazardous to Health
      Regulations 2002 5
cooking and serving food 77–8
COSHH file 102, 105
cross contamination 74–5, 76, 78

D
Data Protection Act 1998 140
dehydration 84–5
disposal of food 78
dysphagia 43–4

E
employees
  hazardous substances 104–5
  Health and Safety at Work Act 1974 4, 12
  legal responsibilities in relation to risk 22
  medication and health care 52–7
  moving and positioning 89–90
  role in reducing spread of infection 64–5
  security 131–3
employers
  agency workers and 8,12
  legal responsibilities in relation to risk 22
  legislation in different settings 6
  liability insurance 8
  moving and positioning 89, 93
  person with disability as 11–12
  reporting accidents and illnesses 38–9
  responsibilities for control of infection 63
  responsibilities for storing, using and disposing of
      hazardous substances 101–2
  responsibility for fire safety 112, 121
  responsibility for health and safety 3, 7, 10–12
  responsibility for security 131
empowerment 28
epilepsy 45–6
equipment and procedures for infection control
      66, 69
Essential Standards of Quality and Safety 6
European Regulation (EC) No 1272/2008 on
      classification, labelling and packaging (CLP)
      103–4
evacuation routes 120–3, 126

F
fire blankets 116, 118
fire extinguishers 115, 116–18
fire safety 108–28
  emergency procedures 119–20
  employee's responsibility 112–14
  employer's responsibility for 112
  equipment 115–18
  escape routes in someone's home 125–7
  evacuation procedures in community settings
      124–5
  evacuation routes 121–4, 126
  for people with learning disabilities 109–10
  guidance for care workers 111
  law and 110–12

personal emergency evacuation plans 124
systems and equipment in public buildings 119
Fire Safety Regulations (Northern Ireland) 2010
    5, 110
Fire Safety (Scotland) Regulations 2006 5, 110
Fire Scotland Act 2005 110
first aid 40–8
    three main aims of 40
Five Steps to Risk Assessment 22
fluid intake, recommended level 83
food hygiene 75–6
food safety 73–87
    coloured chopping boards 76
    cooking and serving food 77–8
    disposing of food 78
    food hygiene 75–6
    food storage 76–7
    legislation 74
Food Safety Act 1990 74
Food Safety Act (Amendment) Regulations 2004 74
food storage 76–7
fractures 47

H
hand hygiene 64, 66–7
hazardous substances and materials 99–101
    disposal of 105
    employee's responsibilities 104–6
    employer's responsibilities 101–2
    in work setting 100
    labelling and information 103–4
    safe practices 101–6
    storage of 103
    working in someone's home 105–6
Health and Safety at Work Act 1974 3–4, 131
    employee's responsibilities 12
    employer's responsibilities 10, 22
Health and Safety Executive (HSE) 5, 6
    Five Steps to Risk Assessment 22
    Guidance on safe handling and positioning 94–5
    risk assessment for hazardous substances 101–2
    two types of risk assessment 90–2
Health and Safety (First-Aid) Regulations 1981
    4, 40
Health and Social Care Act 2008 6, 63
health care tasks 56–7
Healthcare Improvement Scotland 6
Healthcare Inspectorate Wales 6
hydration
    how to promote good 85–6
    importance of 82–3
    signs of dehydration 84–5

I
illness see accidents and sudden illness
Independence, Choice and Risk: A Guide to Best
    Practice in Supported Decision Making 26

infection 61–72
    employee's role in reducing spread of 64
    employer's responsibilities for control of 63
    equipment and infection control 69
    hand hygiene 64, 66–7
    own health and hygiene 70–1
    protective clothing, equipment and procedures
        67–8
    routes by which infection gets into body 62
    safe handling of infected and clinical waste 69–70
    situations that require special management 68
    supporting others to prevent the spread of 65, 68
    working in someone's own home 69
information, access to 140–1
information and support 15

L
legislation 3–5
    access to information 140
    administration and storage of medication 51
    fire safety 110–12
    food safety 74
    hazardous substances 101, 103
    moving and positioning 89
    regulations 4–5
    security and deprivation of liberty 134
Lifting Operations and Lifting Equipment
    Regulations 1998 (LOLER) 4, 93–4
'lone worker' policy 144
loss of consciousness 44–5

M
Management of Health and Safety at Work
    Regulations 1999 (MHSWR) 5, 19, 22
Manual Handling Operations Regulations 1992
    4, 89–92
masks 68
medication 50–61
    employee's responsibilities 52–6
    errors with 59
    legislation regulating 51
    principles relating to safe handling of 53–6
Medication Administration in Social Care 59
medicines, safe handling of 53–6
Medicines Act 1968 51
Medicines and Healthcare Products Regulatory
    Agency (MHRA) Enforcement & Intelligence
    Group (E & I) 51
Medicines Regulatory Group (Northern Ireland) 51
Mental Capacity Act 2005 140
Mental Capacity Act Deprivation of Liberty
    Safeguards (England and Wales) 134
Misuse of Drugs Act 1971 51
Misuse of Drugs (Amendment No 2) (England,
    Wales and Scotland) Regulations 2012 51
Misuse of Drugs (Safe Custody) Regulations 1973
    51

moving and positioning 88–98
  employee's responsibilities 89–90
  employer's responsibilities 89
  legislation 89
  maintaining the person's dignity 95–6
  principles of safe 94–5

N
nutrition 79–82
  complex health and/or particular dietary needs 81–2
  how to promote good 85–6
  importance of 79–80
  people with learning difficulties 81
  religion, culture and food 82
  signs of poor 83–4

O
over-the-counter medication 53

P
PEG feeding 58, 69, 82
person centred approaches, risk assessment 25–6, 30
personal and intimate care 56–7
personal emergency evacuation plans (PEEPs) 124
Personal Protective Equipment at Work Regulations 1992 4, 63
policies and procedures 6–10
  accidents and sudden illness 35–7
  fire safety 113
  medication and health care 51–2
Postural Care Action Group 93
problems with breathing 41–2
protective clothing, equipment and procedures 67–8
Provision and Use of Work Equipment Regulations 1998 (PUWER) 4, 5, 93

R
recording and reporting accidents and illnesses 36, 38–40
recovery position 44–5
Regulation and Quality Improvement Authority (Northern Ireland) 6, 131
regulations see legislation
Regulatory Reform (Fire Safety) Order 2005 5, 110
religion, culture and food 82
Reporting of Injuries, Diseases and Dangerous Occurrences Regulation 1995 (RIDDOR) 4, 38–40
rights, people with learning disabilities and 25
risk 19–32
  assessment in an organisation 23
  assessment in someone's own home 23, 25
  black and minority ethnic communities 27–8

  employee's responsibilities 22
  employer's responsibilities 22
  fire safety assessment 110–12
  importance of assessing 21–3
  people with learning disabilities 25–7
  reporting 23–5
  rights and health and safety concerns 28–30
  'risk and empowerment' divide 28
  two types of assessment 90–2
Royal Pharmaceutical Society 53–4

S
security 129–47
  access for relatives and friends 141–2
  access to information 140–1
  employee's responsibility in work setting 131–3
  employer's responsibilities in the work setting 131
    identity of anyone requesting access to premises or information 139–43
  in an organization 133–4
  in someone's home 132–3, 135–7, 142–3
  locked doors and deprivation of liberty 134
  own security is important 143–5
  people with a learning disability and 133
  people with challenging behaviours 139, 145
  safety when out in the community 137–39, 144
shared responsibilities, health and safety regulation 5–6
stress 148–58
  causes 151–2
  common signs and indicators 149–51
  helping people with learning disabilities manage 156–7
  recognising in other people 152–4
  strategies for managing 154–5
sudden illness see accidents and sudden illness

T
The Handling of Medicines in Social Care 53
training 13–15
  importance of 5
  medication and health care 52–3, 56
  seeking additional information and support 15–16
  tasks not allowed without 14, 37–8, 52, 56, 57–9, 96–7

V
vegetarians, balanced diet for 81

W
waste disposal see clinical waste
Workplace (Health, Safety and Welfare) Regulations 1992 4, 94